Remnants of Auschwitz

Homo Sacer III

Translated by Daniel Heller-Roazen

Remnants of Auschwitz

The Witness and the Archive

Giorgio Agamben

ZONE BOOKS · NEW YORK

2002

First Paperback Edition
Sixth Printing 2018

Printed in the United States of America.

Distributed by The MIT Press,
Cambridge, Massachusetts, and London, England

Library of Congress Cataloging-in-Publication Data

Agamben, Giorgio, 1942-
    [Quel che resta di Auschwitz English.]
    Remnants of Auschwitz : the witness and
the archive / Giorgio Agamben; translated by Daniel
Heller-Roazen.
        p.   cm.
    Includes bibliographical references.
    ISBN 978-1-890951-17-7 (pbk.)
    1. Holocaust, Jewish (1939–1945) — Personal
narratives — History and criticism. 2. Holocaust, Jewish
(1939–1945) — Moral and ethical aspects. 3. Auschwitz
(Concentration camp) 4. Poststructuralism. I. Title.

D804.195.A53 2000
940.53'18 — dc21
                                        99–26013

Contents

In memoriam
Bianca Casalini Agamben
"To be exposed to everything is to be capable of everything."

To Andrea, Daniel, and Guido who, in discussing these pages
with me, allowed them to come to light.

And then it shall come to pass in that day, that the remnant of Israel, and such as are escaped of the house of Jacob, shall no more again stay upon him that smote them; but shall stay upon the Lord, the Holy One of Israel, in truth.

The remnant shall be saved, even the remnant of Jacob, unto the mighty God.

Isaiah 10: 20–22

Even so then at this present time also there is a remnant according to the election of grace .... and so all Israel shall be saved.

Romans 11: 5–26

Preface

Thanks to a series of increasingly wide-ranging and rigorous studies — among which Raul Hilberg's *The Destruction of the European Jews* occupies a special place — the problem of the historical, material, technical, bureaucratic, and legal circumstances in which the extermination of the Jews took place has been sufficiently clarified. Future studies may shed new light on particular aspects of the events that took place in the concentration camps, but a general framework has already been established.

The same cannot be said for the ethical and political significance of the extermination, or even for a human understanding of what happened there — that is, for its contemporary relevance. Not only do we lack anything close to a complete understanding; even the sense and reasons for the behavior of the executioners and the victims, indeed very often their very words, still seem profoundly enigmatic. This can only encourage the opinion of those who would like Auschwitz to remain forever incomprehensible.

From a historical perspective, we know, for example, the most minute details of how the final phase of the extermination was executed, how the deportees were led to the gas chambers by a squad of their fellow inmates (the so-called *Sonderkommando*), who then saw to it that the corpses were dragged out and washed, that their hair and gold teeth were salvaged, and that their bodies, finally, were placed in the crematoria. We can enumerate and describe each of these events, but they remain singularly opaque when we truly seek to understand them. This discrepancy and unease has perhaps never been described more directly than by Zelman Lewental, a member of the *Sonderkommando* who entrusted his testimony to a few sheets of paper buried under crematorium III, which came to light seventeen years after the liberation of Auschwitz. "Just as the events that took place there cannot be imagined by any human being," Lewental writes in Yiddish, "so is it unimaginable that anyone could exactly recount how our experiences took place.... we, the small group of obscure people who will not give historians much work to do."

What is at issue here is not, of course, the difficulty we face whenever we try to communicate our most intimate experiences to others. The discrepancy in question concerns the very structure of testimony. On the one hand, what happened in the camps appears to the survivors as the only true thing and, as such, absolutely unforgettable; on the other hand, this truth is to the same degree unimaginable, that is, irreducible to the real elements that constitute it. Facts so real that, by comparison, nothing is truer; a reality that necessarily exceeds its factual elements — such is the aporia of Auschwitz. As Lewental writes, "the complete truth is far more tragic, far more frightening...." More tragic, more frightening than what?

Lewental had it wrong on at least one point. There is no doubt that "the small group of obscure people" ("obscure" here is to be understood in the literal sense as invisible, that which cannot be perceived) will continue to give historians work to do. The aporia of Auschwitz is, indeed, the very aporia of historical knowledge: a non-coincidence between facts and truth, between verification and comprehension.

Some want to understand too much and too quickly; they have explanations for everything. Others refuse to understand; they offer only cheap mystifications. The only way forward lies in investigating the space between these two options. Moreover, a further difficulty must be considered, one which is particularly important for anyone who studies literary or philosophical texts. Many testimonies — both of executioners and victims — come from ordinary people, the "obscure" people who clearly comprised the great majority of camp inhabitants. One of the lessons of Auschwitz is that it is infinitely harder to grasp the mind of an ordinary person than to understand the mind of a Spinoza or Dante. (Hannah Arendt's discussion of the "banality of evil," so often misunderstood, must also be understood in this sense.)

Some readers may be disappointed to find that there is little in this book that cannot already be found in the testimonies of survivors. In its form, this book is a kind of perpetual commentary on testimony. It did not seem possible to proceed otherwise. At a certain point, it became clear that testimony contained at its core an essential lacuna; in other words, the survivors bore witness to something it is impossible to bear witness to. As a consequence, commenting on survivors' testimony necessarily meant interrogating this lacuna or, more precisely, attempting to listen to it. Listening to something absent did not prove fruitless work for this author. Above all, it made it necessary to clear away almost all the doctrines that, since Auschwitz, have been advanced in the name of ethics. As we shall see, almost none of the ethical principles our age believed it could recognize as valid have stood the decisive test, that of an *Ethica more Auschwitz demonstrata*. For my own part, I will consider myself content with my work if, in attempting to locate the place and theme of testimony, I have erected some signposts allowing future cartographers of the new ethical territory to orient themselves. Indeed, I will be satisfied if this book succeeds only in correcting some of the terms with which we register the decisive lesson of the century and if this book makes it possible for certain words to be left behind and others to be understood in a different sense. This is also a way — perhaps the only way — to listen to what is unsaid.

CHAPTER ONE

The Witness

1. 1   In the camp, <u>one of the reasons that can drive a prisoner to survive is the idea of becoming a witness.</u> "I firmly decided that, despite everything that might happen to me, I would not take my own life ... since I did not want to suppress the witness that I could become" (Langbein 1988: 186). Of course, not all deportees, indeed only a small fraction of them, give this reason. A reason for survival can be a matter of <u>convenience:</u> "He would like to survive for this or that reason, for this or that end, and he finds hundreds of pretexts. The truth is that he wants to live at whatever cost" (Lewental 1972: 148). Or it can simply be a matter of <u>revenge:</u> "Naturally I could have run and thrown myself onto the fence, because you can always do that. But I want to live. And what if the miracle happens we're all waiting for? Maybe we'll be liberated, today or tomorrow. Then I'll have my revenge, then I'll tell the whole world what happened here — inside there" (Sofsky 1997: 340). To justify one's survival is not easy — least of all in the camp. Then there are some survivors who prefer to be silent. "Some of my friends, very dear friends of mine, never speak of Auschwitz" (Levi 1997: 224). Yet, for others, the only reason to live is to ensure that the witness does not perish. "Others, on the other hand, speak of it incessantly, and I am one of them" (*ibid.*).

1.2   Primo Levi is a perfect example of the witness. When he returns home, he tirelessly recounts his experience to everyone. He behaves like Coleridge's Ancient Mariner:

> You remember the scene: the Ancient Mariner accosts the wedding guests, who are thinking of the wedding and not paying attention to him, and he forces them to listen to his tale. Well, when I first returned from the concentration camp I did just that. I felt an unrestrainable need to tell my story to anyone and everyone!... Every situation was an occasion to tell my story to anyone and everyone: to tell it to the factory director as well as to the worker, even if they had other things to do. I was reduced to the state of the Ancient Mariner. Then I began to write on my typewriter at night.... Every night I would write, and this was considered even crazier! (Levi 1997: 224–25)

But Levi does not consider himself a writer; he becomes a writer so that he can bear witness. In a sense, he never became a writer. In 1963, after publishing two novels and many short stories, he responds unhesitatingly to the question of whether he considers himself a writer or a chemist: "A chemist, of course, let there be no mistake" (Levi 1997: 102). Levi was profoundly uneasy with the fact that as time passed, and almost in spite of himself, he ended up a writer, composing books that had nothing to do with his testimony: "Then I wrote.... I acquired the vice of writing" (Levi 1997: 258). "In my latest book, *La Chiave a stella*, I stripped myself completely of my status as a witness.... This is not to deny anything; I have not ceased to be an ex-deportee, a witness...." (*ibid.*: 167)

Levi had this unease about him when I saw him at meetings at the Italian publisher, Einaudi. He could feel guilty for having survived, but not for having borne witness. "I am at peace with myself because I bore witness" (*ibid.*: p. 219).

1.3　In Latin there are two words for "witness." The first word, *testis*, from which our word "testimony" derives, etymologically signifies the person who, in a trial or lawsuit between two rival parties, is in the position of a third party (*terstis). The second word, *superstes*, designates a person who has lived through something, who has experienced an event from beginning to end and can therefore bear witness to it. It is obvious that Levi is not a third party; he is a survivor [*superstite*] in every sense. But this also means that his testimony has nothing to do with the acquisition of facts for a trial (he is not neutral enough for this, he is not a *testis*). In the final analysis, it is not judgment that matters to him, let alone pardon. "I never appear as judge"; "I do not have the authority to grant pardon.... I am without authority" (*ibid.*: 77, 236). It seems, in fact, that the only thing that interests him is what makes judgment impossible: the gray zone in which victims become executioners and executioners become victims. It is about this above all that the survivors are in agreement: "No group was more human than any other" (*ibid.*: 232). "Victim and executioner are equally ignoble; the lesson of the camps is brotherhood in abjection" (Rousset, cf. Levi 1997: 216).

Not that a judgment cannot or must not be made. "If I had had Eichmann before me, I would have condemned him to death" (*ibid.*: 144). "If they have committed a crime, then they must pay" (*ibid.*: 236). The decisive point is simply that the two things not be blurred, that law not presume to exhaust the question. A nonjuridical element of truth exists such that the *quaestio facti* can never be reduced to the *quaestio iuris*. This is precisely what concerns the survivor: everything that places a human action beyond the law, radically withdrawing it from the Trial. "Each of us can

be tried, condemned and punished without even knowing why"
(*ibid.*: 75).

1.4   One of the most common mistakes — which is not only made
in discussions of the camp — is the tacit confusion of ethical categories and juridical categories (or, worse, of juridical categories
and theological categories, which gives rise to a new theodicy).
Almost all the categories that we use in moral and religious judgments are in some way contaminated by law: guilt, responsibility,
innocence, judgment, pardon.... This makes it difficult to invoke
them without particular caution. As jurists well know, law is not
directed toward the establishment of justice. Nor is it directed
toward the verification of truth. Law is solely directed toward
judgment, independent of truth and justice. This is shown beyond
doubt by the *force of judgment* that even an unjust sentence carries
with it. The ultimate aim of law is the production of a *res judicata*,
in which the sentence becomes the substitute for the true and the
just, being held as true despite its falsity and injustice. Law finds
peace in this hybrid creature, of which it is impossible to say if it
is fact or rule; once law has produced its *res judicata*, it cannot go
any further.

In 1983, the publisher Einaudi asked Levi to translate Kafka's
The Trial. Infinite interpretations of *The Trial* have been offered;
some underline the novel's prophetic political character (modern
bureaucracy as absolute evil) or its theological dimension (the
court as the unknown God) or its biographical meaning (condemnation as the illness from which Kafka believed himself to suffer).
It has been rarely noted that this book, in which law appears
solely in the form of a trial, contains a profound insight into the
nature of law, which, contrary to common belief, is not so much
rule as it is judgment and, therefore, trial. But if the essence of
the law — of every law — is the trial, if all right (and morality that

is contaminated by it) is only tribunal right, then execution and transgression, innocence and guilt, obedience and disobedience all become indistinct and lose their importance. "The court wants nothing from you. It welcomes you when you come; it releases you when you go." The ultimate end of the juridical regulation is to produce judgment; but judgment aims neither to punish nor to extol, neither to establish justice nor to prove the truth. Judgment is in itself the end and this, it has been said, constitutes its mystery, the mystery of the trial.

One of the consequences that can be drawn from this self-referential nature of judgment — and Sebastiano Satta, a great Italian jurist, has done so — is that punishment does not follow from judgment, but rather that judgment is itself punishment (*nullum judicium sine poena*). "One can even say that the whole punishment is in the judgment, that the action characteristic of the punishment — incarceration, execution — matters only insofar as it is, so to speak, the carrying out of the judgment" (Satta 1994: 26). This also means that "the sentence of acquittal is the confession of a judicial error," that "everyone is inwardly innocent," but that the only truly innocent person "is not the one who is acquitted, but rather the one who goes through life without judgment" (*ibid.*: 27).

1. 5   If this is true — and the survivor knows that it is true — then it is possible that the trials (the twelve trials at Nuremberg, and the others that took place in and outside German borders, including those in Jerusalem in 1961 that ended with the hanging of Eichmann) are responsible for the conceptual confusion that, for decades, has made it impossible to think through Auschwitz. Despite the necessity of the trials and despite their evident insufficiency (they involved only a few hundred people), they helped to spread the idea that the problem of Auschwitz had been overcome. The judgments had been passed, the proofs of guilt definitively established.

With the exception of occasional moments of lucidity, it has taken almost half a century to understand that law did not exhaust the problem, but rather that the very problem was so enormous as to call into question law itself, dragging it to its own ruin.

The confusion between law and morality and between theology and law has had illustrious victims. Hans Jonas, the philosopher and student of Heidegger who specialized in ethical problems, is one of them. In 1984, when he received the Lucas Award in Tübingen, he reflected on the question of Auschwitz by preparing for a new theodicy, asking, that is, how it was possible for God to tolerate Auschwitz. A theodicy is a trial that seeks to establish the responsibility not of men, but of God. Like all theodicies, Jonas's ends in an acquittal. The justification for the sentence is something like this: "The infinite (God) stripped himself completely, in the finite, of his omnipotence. Creating the world, God gave it His own fate and became powerless. Thus, having emptied himself entirely in the world, he no longer has anything to offer us; it is now man's turn to give. Man can do this by taking care that it never happens, or rarely happens, that God regrets his decision to have let the world be."

The conciliatory vice of every theodicy is particularly clear here. Not only does this theodicy tell us nothing about Auschwitz, either about its victims or executioners; it does not even manage to avoid a happy ending. Behind the powerlessness of God peeps the powerlessness of men, who continue to cry "May that never happen again!" when it is clear that "that" is, by now, everywhere.

1.6   The concept of responsibility is also irremediably contaminated by law. Anyone who has tried to make use of it outside the juridical sphere knows this. And yet ethics, politics, and religion have been able to define themselves only by seizing terrain from juridical responsibility — not in order to assume another kind of responsibility, but to articulate zones of non-responsibility. This does not, of course, mean impunity. Rather, it signifies — at least for ethics — a confrontation with a responsibility that is infinitely greater than any we could ever assume. At the most, we can be faithful to it, that is, assert its unassumability.

The unprecedented discovery made by Levi at Auschwitz concerns an area that is independent of every establishment of responsibility, an area in which Levi succeeded in isolating something like a new ethical element. Levi calls it the "gray zone." It is the zone in which the "long chain of conjunction between victim and executioner" comes loose, where the oppressed becomes oppressor and the executioner in turn appears as victim. A gray, incessant alchemy in which good and evil and, along with them, all the metals of traditional ethics reach their point of fusion.

What is at issue here, therefore, is a zone of irresponsibility and "*impotentia judicandi*" (Levi 1989: 60) that is situated not *beyond* good and evil but rather, so to speak, *before* them. With a gesture that is symmetrically opposed to that of Nietzsche, Levi places ethics before the area in which we are accustomed to consider it. And, without our being able to say why, we sense that this "before" is more important than any "beyond" — that the "underman" must matter to us more than the "overman." This infamous zone of irresponsibility is our First Circle, from which no confession of responsibility will remove us and in which what is spelled out, minute by minute, is the lesson of the "terrifying, unsayable and unimaginable banality of evil" (Arendt 1992: 252).

1.7   The Latin verb *spondeo*, which is the origin of our term "responsibility," means "to become the guarantor of something for someone (or for oneself) with respect to someone." Thus, in the promise of marriage, the father would utter the formula *spondeo* to express his commitment to giving his daughter as wife to a suitor (after which she was then called a *sponsa*) or to guarantee compensation if this did not take place. In archaic Roman law, in fact, the custom was that a free man could consign himself as a hostage — that is, in a state of imprisonment, from which the term *obligatio* derives — to guarantee the compensation of a wrong or the fulfillment of an obligation. (The term *sponsor* indicated the person who substituted himself for the *reus*, promising, in the case of a breach of contract, to furnish the required service.)

The gesture of assuming responsibility is therefore genuinely juridical and not ethical. It expresses nothing noble or luminous, but rather simply obligation, the act by which one consigned oneself as a prisoner to guarantee a debt in a context in which the legal bond was considered to inhere in the body of the person responsible. As such, responsibility is closely intertwined with the concept of *culpa* that, in a broad sense, indicates the imputability of damage. (This is why the Romans denied that there could be guilt with respect to oneself: *quod quis ex culpa sua damnum sentit, non intelligitur damnum sentire*: the damage that one causes to oneself by one's own fault is not juridically relevant.)

Responsibility and guilt thus express simply two aspects of legal imputability; only later were they interiorized and moved outside law. Hence the insufficiency and opacity of every ethical doctrine that claims to be founded on these two concepts. (This holds both for Jonas, who claimed to formulate a genuine "principle of responsibility" and for Lévinas, who, in a much more complex fashion, transformed the gesture of the *sponsor* into the ethical gesture par excellence.) This insufficiency and opacity emerges clearly every time the borders that separate ethics from law are traced. Let us consider two examples, which are very far from each other as to the gravity of the facts they concern but which coincide with respect to the *distinguo* they imply.

22

During the Jerusalem trial, Eichmann's constant line of defense was clearly expressed by his lawyer, Robert Serviatus, with these words: "Eichmann feels himself guilty before God, not the law." Eichmann (whose implication in the extermination of the Jews was well documented, even if his role was probably different from that which was argued by the prosecution) actually went so far as to declare that he wanted "to hang himself in public" in order to "liberate young Germans from the weight of guilt." Yet, until the end, he continued to maintain that his guilt before God (who was for him only a *höherer Sinnesträger*, a higher bearer of meaning) could not be legally prosecuted. The only possible explanation for this insistence is that, whereas the assumption of moral guilt seemed ethically noble to the defendant, he was unwilling to assume any legal guilt (although, from an ethical point of view, legal guilt should have been less serious than moral guilt).

Recently, a group of people who once had belonged to a political organization of the extreme Left published a communiqué in a newspaper, declaring political and moral responsibility for the murder of a police officer committed twenty years ago. "Nevertheless, such responsibility," the document stated, "cannot be transformed ... into a responsibility of penal character." It must be recalled that the assumption of moral responsibility has value only if one is ready to assume the relevant legal consequences. The authors of the communiqué seem to suspect this in some way, when, in a significant passage, they assume a responsibility that sounds unmistakably juridical, stating that they contributed to "creating a climate that led to murder." (But the offense in question, the instigation to commit a crime, is of course wiped out.) In every age, the gesture of assuming a juridical responsibility when one is innocent has been considered noble; the assumption of political or moral responsibility without the assumption of the corresponding legal consequences, on the other hand, has always characterized the arrogance of the mighty (consider Mussolini's behavior, for example, with respect to the case of Giacomo Matteotti, the member of the Italian parliament who was assassinated by unknown killers in 1924). But today in Italy these models have been reversed and the contrite assumption of moral responsibilities is invoked at every occasion as an exemption from the responsibilities demanded by law.

Here the confusion between ethical categories and juridical categories (with the logic of repentance implied) is absolute. This confusion lies at the origin of the many suicides committed to escape trial (not only those of Nazi criminals), in which the tacit assumption of moral guilt attempts to compensate for legal guilt. It is worth remembering that the primary responsibility for this confusion lies not in Catholic doctrine, which includes a sacrament whose function is to free the sinner of guilt, but rather in secular ethics (in its well-meaning and dominant version). After having raised juridical categories to the status of supreme ethical categories and thereby irredeemably confusing the fields of law ethics, secular ethics still wants to play out its *distinguo*. But ethics is the sphere that recognizes neither guilt nor responsibility; it is, as Spinoza knew, the doctrine of the happy life. To assume guilt and responsibility — which can, at times, be necessary — is to leave the territory of ethics and enter that of law. Whoever has made this difficult step cannot presume to return through the door he just closed behind him.

1.8 The extreme figure of the "gray zone" is the *Sonderkommando*. The SS used the euphemism "special team" to refer to this group of deportees responsible for managing the gas chambers and crematoria. Their task was to lead naked prisoners to their death in the gas chambers and maintain order among them; they then had to drag out the corpses, stained pink and green by the cyanotic acid, and wash them with water; make sure that no valuable objects were hidden in the orifices of the bodies; extract gold teeth from the corpses' jaws; cut the women's hair and wash it with ammonia chloride; bring the corpses into the crematoria and oversee their incineration; and, finally, empty out the ovens of the ash that remained. Levi writes:

> Concerning these squads, vague and mangled rumors already circulated among us during our imprisonment and were confirmed afterward.... But the intrinsic horror of this human condition has imposed a sort of reserve on all the testimony, so that even today it is difficult to conjure up an image of "what it meant" to be forced to exercise this trade for months.... One of them declared: "Doing this work, one either goes crazy the first day or gets accustomed to it." Another, though: "Certainly, I could have killed myself or got myself killed; but I wanted to survive, to avenge myself and bear witness. You mustn't think that we are monsters; we are the same as you, only much more unhappy."... One cannot expect from men who have known such extreme destitution a deposition in the juridical sense, but something that is at once a lament, a curse, an expiation, an attempt to justify and rehabilitate oneself.... Conceiving and organizing the squads was National Socialism's most demonic crime (Levi 1989: 52–3).

And yet Levi recalls that a witness, Miklos Nyszli, one of the very few who survived the last "special team" of Auschwitz, recounted that during a "work" break he took part in a soccer match between the SS and representatives of the *Sonderkommando*. "Other men of the SS and the rest of the squad are present at the game; they take sides, bet, applaud, urge the players on as if, rather than at the gates of hell, the game were taking place on the village green" (Levi 1989: 55).

This match might strike someone as a brief pause of humanity in the middle of an infinite horror. I, like the witnesses, instead view this match, this moment of normalcy, as the true horror of the camp. For we can perhaps think that the massacres are over — even if here and there they are repeated, not so far away from us. But that match is never over; it continues as if uninterrupted. It is the perfect and eternal cipher of the "gray zone," which knows no time and is in every place. Hence the anguish and shame of the survivors, "the anguish inscribed in everyone of the 'tohu-bohu,' of a deserted and empty universe crushed under the spirit of God but from which the spirit of man is absent: not yet born or already extinguished" (Levi 1989: 85). But also hence our shame, the shame of those who did not know the camps and yet, without knowing how, are spectators of that match, which repeats itself in every match in our stadiums, in every television broadcast, in the normalcy of everyday life. If we do not succeed in understanding that match, in stopping it, there will never be hope.

1.9   In Greek the word for witness is *martis*, martyr. The first Church Fathers coined the word *martirium* from *martis* to indicate the death of persecuted Christians, who thus bore witness to their faith. What happened in the camps has little to do with martyrdom. The survivors are unanimous about this. "By calling the victims of the Nazis 'martyrs,' we falsify their fate" (Bettelheim 1979: 92). Nevertheless, the concepts of "witnessing" and "martyrdom" can be linked in two ways. The first concerns the Greek term itself, derived as it is from the verb meaning "to remember." The survivor's vocation is to remember; he cannot *not* remember. "The memories of my imprisonment are much more vivid and detailed than those of anything else that happened to me before or after" (Levi 1997: 225). "I still have a visual and acoustic memory of the experiences there that I cannot explain.... sentences in languages I do not know have remained etched in my memory, like on a magnetic tape; I have repeated them to Poles and Hungarians and have been told that the sentences are meaningful. For some reason that I cannot explain, something anomalous happened to me, I would say almost an unconscious preparation for bearing witness" (*ibid.:* 220).

The second point of connection is even more profound, more instructive. The study of the first Christian texts on martyrdom — for example, Tertullian's *Scorpiacus* — reveals some unexpected teachings. The Church Fathers were confronted by heretical groups that rejected martyrdom because, in their eyes, it constituted a wholly senseless death (*perire sine causa*). What meaning could be found in professing one's faith before men — persecutors and executioners — who would understand nothing of this undertaking? God could not desire something without meaning. "Must innocents suffer these things?... Once and for all Christ immolated himself for us; once and for all he was killed, precisely so that we would not be killed. If he asks for the same in return, is it perhaps because he too expects salvation in my death? Or should one perhaps think that God demands the blood of men even while he disdains that of bulls and goats? How could God ever desire the death of someone who is not a sinner?" The doctrine of martyrdom therefore justifies the scandal of a meaningless death, of an execution that could only appear as absurd. Confronted with the spectacle of a death that was apparently *sine causa*, the reference to Luke 12: 8–9 and to Matthew 10: 32–33 ("Whosoever therefore shall confess me before men, him will I confess also before my Father which is in heaven. But whosoever shall deny me before men, him will I also deny before my Father which is in heaven") made it possible to interpret martyrdom as a divine command and, thus, to find a reason for the irrational.

But this has very much to do with the camps. For what appears in the camps is an extermination for which it may be possible to find precedents, but whose forms make it absolutely senseless. Survivors are also in agreement on this. "Even to us, what we had to tell would start to seem *unimaginable*" (Antelme 1992: 3). "All the attempts at clarification...failed ridiculously" (Améry 1980: vii). "I am irritated by the attempts of some religious extremists to interpret the extermination according to the manner of the prophets: as a punishment for our sins. No! I do not accept this. What is terrifying is that it was senseless...." (Levi 1997: 219).

The unfortunate term "holocaust" (usually with a capital "H") arises from this unconscious demand to justify a death that is *sine causa* — to give meaning back to what seemed incomprehensible. "Please excuse me, I use this term 'Holocaust' reluctantly because I do not like it. But I use it to be understood. Philologically, it is a mistake...." (*ibid.*: 243). "It is a term that, when it first arose, gave me a lot of trouble; then I learned that it was Wiesel himself who had coined it, then regretted it and wanted to take it back" (*ibid.*: 219).

1.10   The history of an incorrect term can also prove instructive. "Holocaust" is the scholarly transcription of the Latin *holocaustum* which, in turn, is a translation of the Greek term *holocaustos* (which is, however, an adjective, and which means "completely burned"; the corresponding Greek noun is *holocaustōma*). The semantic history of the term is essentially Christian, since the Church Fathers used it to translate — in fact with neither rigour nor coherence — the complex sacrificial doctrine of the Bible (in particular, of Leviticus and Deuteronomy). Leviticus reduces all sacrifices to four fundamental types: *olah, hattat, shelamin, minha*. As Marcel Mauss and Henri Hubert write in "The Nature and Function of Sacrifice,"

The names of two of these are significant. The *hattat* was the sacrifice employed especially to expiate the sin called *hattat* or *hataah*, the definition of which given in Leviticus is unfortunately extremely vague. The *shelamin* is a communion sacrifice, a sacrifice of thanksgiving, of alliance, of vows. As for the terms *'olah* and *minha*, they are purely descriptive. Each recalls one of the special operations of sacrifice: the latter, the presentation of the victim, if it is of vegetable matter, the former, the dispatch of the offering to the divinity (Mauss and Hubert 1964: 16).

The Vulgate usually translates *olah* by *holocaustum* (*holocausti oblatio*); *hattat* by *oblatio*; *shelamin* by *hostia pacificorum*; *minha* by *hostia pro peccato*. The term *holocaustum* is transmitted from the Vulgate to the Latin Fathers, who used it primarily in the many commentaries of the Holy Writ to indicate the sacrifices of the Hebrews. (Thus in Hilarius, *In Psalmata*, 65, 23: *holocausta sunt integra hostiarum corpora, quia tota ad ignem sacrificii deferebantur, holocausta sunt nuncupata*.) Two points are particularly important here. First, early on, the Church Fathers used the term in its literal sense as a polemical weapon against the Jews, to condemn the uselessness of bloody sacrifices (Tertullian's text, which refers to Marcion, is exemplary: *Quid stultius.... quam sacrificiorum cruentorum et holocaustomatum nidorosurum a deo exactio?* "What is more foolish than a god who demands bloody sacrifices and holocausts that smell of burnt remains?" *Adversus Marcionem* 5, 5; cf. also Augustine, *C. Faustusm*, 19, 4). Second, the term "holocaustum" is extended as a metaphor to include Christian martyrs, such that their torture is equated with sacrifice (Hilarius, *In Psalmata*, 65, 23: *Martyres in fidei testimonium corpora sua holocausta voverunt*). Christ's sacrifice on the cross is thus ultimately defined as a holocaust (Augustine, *In Evang. Joah.*, 41, 5: *se in holocaustum obtulerit in cruce Iesus*; Rufinus,

Origines in Leviticum, 1, 4: *holocaustum.... carnis eius per lignum crucis oblatum*).

Thus begins the semantic migration by which the term "holo-caust" in vernacular languages gradually acquires the meaning of the "supreme sacrifice in the sphere of a complete devotion to sacred and superior motives." In English, the term appears in its literal sense in Tindale (*Mark* xii. 33: "A greater thynge than all holocaustes and sacrifises") and H. More (*Apocal. Apoc.* 101: "In the latter part thereof stands the altar of Holocausts"). The term appears in its metaphorical sense in Bp. Alcock (*Mons Perfect* C iija: "Very true obedyence is an holocauste of martyrdom made to Cryste"), J. Beaumont (*Psyche* xxiv. cxciv: "The perfect holocaust of generous love") and Milton, where it signifies a complete con-sumption by fire (*Samson* 1702: "Like that self-begotten bird In the Arabian woods embost, That no second knows nor third, And lay erewhile a Holocaust"). It is repeated, over and over again, through to the twentieth century (for example, *Hansard Commons* 6 March, 1940: "the general holocaust of civilized standards") (*Oxford English Dictionary* 1989: 315).

But the term's usage in polemics against the Jews also has a history, even if it is a secret one not recorded by dictionaries. In the course of my research on sovereignty, I happened upon a pas-sage by a medieval chronicler that constitutes, to my knowledge, the first use of *holocaust* with reference to a massacre of Jews, in this case in a violently anti-Semitic fashion. Richard of Duizes tes-tifies that on the day of the coronation of Richard I (1189), the inhabitants of London engaged in a particularly bloody pogrom: "The very day of the coronation of the king, at about the hour in which the Son was burnt for the Father, they began in London to burn the Jews for their father the demon (*incoeptum est in civitate Londoniae immolare judaeos patri suo diabolo*); and the celebration of this mystery lasted so long that the holocaust could not be completed before the next day. And the other cities and towns of the region imitated the faith of the inhabitants of London and, with the same devotion, sent their bloodsuckers to hell (*pari devotione suas sanguisugas cum sanguine transmiserunt ad inferos*)" (Cardini 1994: 131).

Insofar as it implies the substitution of a literal expression with an attenuated or altered expression for something that one does not actually want to hear mentioned, the formation of a euphemism always involves ambiguities. In this case, however, the ambiguity is intolerable. The Jews also use a euphemism to indicate the extermination. They use the term *so'ah*, which means "devastation, catastrophe" and, in the Bible, often implies the idea of a divine punishment (as in Isaiah 10:3: "What will you do in the day of punishment, when the *so'ah* will come from afar?"). Even if Levi probably refers to this term when he speaks of the attempt to interpret the extermination as a punishment for our sins, his use of the euphemism contains no mockery. In the case of the term "holocaust," by contrast, the attempt to establish a connection, however distant, between Auschwitz and the Biblical *olah* and between death in the gas chamber and the "complete devotion to sacred and superior motives" cannot but sound like a jest. Not only does the term imply an unacceptable equation between crematoria and altars; it also continues a semantic heredity that is from its inception anti-Semitic. This is why we will never make use of this term.

1.11 Several years ago, when I published an article on the concentration camps in a French newspaper, someone wrote a letter to the editor in which, among other crimes, I was accused of having sought to "ruin the unique and unsayable character of Auschwitz." I have often asked myself what the author of the letter could have had in mind. The phenomenon of Auschwitz is unique (certainly in the past, and we can only hope for the future). As Levi points out: "Up to the moment of this writing, and notwithstanding the horror of Hiroshima and Nagasaki, the shame of the Gulags, the useless and bloody Vietnam war, the Cambodian self-genocide, the *desaparecidos* in Argentina, and the many atrocious and stupid wars we have seen since, the Nazi concentration camp still remains an *unicum*, both in its extent and its quality" (Levi 1989: 21). But why unsayable? Why confer on extermination the prestige of the mystical?

In the year 386 of our era, in Antioch, John Chrysostom composed his treatise *On the Incomprehensible Nature of God*. He opposed those who maintained that God's essence could be understood, on the grounds that "everything that He knows of Himself we can also easily find in ourselves." Vigorously arguing against his adversaries in affirming the incomprehensibility of God, who is "unsayable" (*arrētos*), "unspeakable" (*anekdiēgētos*), and "unwritable" (*anepigraptos*), John well knew that this was precisely the best way to glorify (*doxan didonai*) and adore (*proskuein*) Him. Even for the angels, after all, God is incomprehensible; but because of this they can glorify and adore Him, offering Him their mystical songs. John contrasts the angelic hosts with those seeking in vain to understand God: "those ones [the angels] glorify, these ones seek to understand; those ones adore in silence, these ones give themselves work to do; those ones divert their gaze, these ones are not ashamed to stare into unsayable glory" (Chrysostom 1970). The verb that we have translated "to adore in silence" is, in the Greek text, *euphemein*. *Euphemein*, which originally means "to observe religious silence," is the origin of the modern word "euphemism," which denotes those terms that are substituted for other terms that cannot be uttered for reasons of modesty or civility. To say that Auschwitz is "unsayable" or "incomprehensible" is equivalent to *euphemein*, to adoring in silence, as one

32

does with a god. Regardless of one's intentions, this contributes to its glory. We, however, "are not ashamed of staring into the unsayable" — even at the risk of discovering that what evil knows of itself, we can also easily find in ourselves.

1.12 Testimony, however, contains a lacuna. The survivors agree about this. "There is another lacuna in every testimony: witnesses are by definition survivors and so all, to some degree, enjoyed a privilege.... No one has told the destiny of the common prisoner, since it was not materially possible for him to survive.... I have also described the common prisoner when I speak of 'Muslims'; but the Muslims did not speak" (Levi 1997: 215–16). "Those who have not lived through the experience will never know; those who have will never tell; not really, not completely.... The past belongs to the dead...." (Wiesel 1975: 314).

It is worth reflecting upon this lacuna, which calls into question the very meaning of testimony and, along with it, the identity and reliability of the witnesses. "I must repeat: we, the survivors, are not the true witnesses.... We survivors are not only an exiguous but also an anomalous minority: we are those who by their prevarications or abilities or good luck did not touch bottom. Those who did so, those who saw the Gorgon, have not returned to tell about it or have returned mute, but they are the Muslims, the submerged, the complete witnesses, the ones whose deposition would have a general significance. They are the rule, we are the exception.... We who were favored by fate tried, with more or less wisdom, to recount not only our fate but also that of the others, indeed of the drowned; but this was a discourse 'on behalf of third parties,' the story of things seen at close hand, not experienced personally. The destruction brought to an end, the job completed, was not told by anyone, just as no one ever returned to describe his own death. Even if they had paper and

33

pen, the drowned would not have testified because their death had begun before that of their body. Weeks and months before being snuffed out, they had already lost the ability to observe, to remember, to compare and express themselves. We speak in their stead, by proxy" (Levi 1989: 83–4).

The witness usually testifies in the name of justice and truth and as such his or her speech draws consistency and fullness. Yet here the value of testimony lies essentially in what it lacks; at its center it contains something that cannot be borne witness to and that discharges the survivors of authority. The "true" witnesses, the "complete witnesses," are those who did not bear witness and could not bear witness. They are those who "touched bottom": the Muslims, the drowned. The survivors speak in their stead, by proxy, as pseudo-witnesses; they bear witness to a missing testimony. And yet to speak here of a proxy makes no sense; the drowned have nothing to say, nor do they have instructions or memories to be transmitted. They have no "story" (Levi 1986: 90), no "face," and even less do they have "thought" (*ibid.*). Whoever assumes the charge of bearing witness in their name knows that he or she must bear witness in the name of the impossibility of bearing witness. But this alters the value of testimony in a definitive way; it makes it necessary to look for its meaning in an unexpected area.

1.13   It has already been observed that, in testimony, there is something like an impossibility of bearing witness. In 1983, Jean-François Lyotard published *The Differend*, which, ironically repeating the recent claims of revisionists, opens with a logical paradox:

> You are informed that human beings endowed with language were placed in a situation such that none of them is now able to tell about it. Most of them disappeared then, and the survivors rarely speak

about it. When they do speak about it, their testimony bears only upon a minute part of this situation. How can you know that the situation itself existed? That it is not the fruit of your informant's imagination? Either the situation did not exist as such. Or else it did exist, in which case your informant's testimony is false, either because he or she should have disappeared, or else because he or she should remain silent.... To have "really seen with his own eyes" a gas chamber would be the condition which gives one the authority to say that it exists and to persuade the unbeliever. Yet it is still necessary to prove that the gas chamber was used to kill at the time it was seen. The only acceptable proof that it was used to kill is that one died from it. But if one is dead, one cannot testify that it is on account of the gas chamber (Lyotard 1988: 3).

A few years later, Shoshana Felman and Dori Laub elaborated the notion of the Shoah as an "event without witnesses." In 1990, one of the authors further developed this concept in the form of a commentary on Claude Lanzmann's film. The Shoah is an event without witnesses in the double sense that it is impossible to bear witness to it from the inside — since no one can bear witness from the inside of death, and there is no voice for the disappearance of voice — and from the outside — since the "outsider" is by definition excluded from the event:

It is not really possible to *tell the truth*, to testify, from the outside. Neither is it possible, as we have seen, to testify from the inside. I would suggest that the impossible position and the testimonial effort of the film as a whole is to be, precisely, neither simply inside nor simply outside, but paradoxically, *both inside and outside*: to create a *connection* that did not exist during the war and does not exist today *between the inside and the outside* — to set them both in motion and in dialogue with one another (Felman and Laub 1992: 232).

35

This threshold of indistinction between inside and outside (which, as we shall see, is anything but a "connection" or a "dialogue") could have led to a comprehension of the structure of testimony; yet it is precisely this threshold that Felman fails to interrogate. Instead of developing her pertinent analysis, the author derives an aesthetic possibility from a logical impossibility, through recourse to the metaphor of song:

> What makes the power of the testimony in the film and what constitutes in general the impact of the film is not the words but the equivocal, puzzling relation between words and voice, the interaction, that is, between words, voice, rhythm, melody, images, writing, and silence. Each testimony speaks to us beyond its words, beyond its melody, like the unique performance of a singing (*ibid.*: 277–78).

To explain the paradox of testimony through the deus ex machina of song is to aestheticize testimony — something that Lanzmann is careful to avoid. Neither the poem nor the song can intervene to save impossible testimony; on the contrary, it is testimony, if anything, that founds the possibility of the poem.

1.14 The incomprehension of an honest mind is often instructive. Primo Levi, who did not like obscure authors, was attracted to the poetry of Paul Celan, even if he did not truly succeed in understanding it. In a brief essay, entitled "On Obscure Writing," he distinguishes Celan from those who write obscurely out of contempt for the reader or lack of expressivity. The obscurity of Celan's poetics makes Levi think instead of a "pre-suicide, a not-wanting-to-be, a flight from the world for which a willed death appears as completion." The extraordinary operation accomplished by Celan on the German language, which has so fascinated Celan's readers, is compared by Levi — for reasons worth reflecting on — to an inarticulate babble or the gasps of a dying man. "This darkness that grows from page to page until the last inarticulate babble fills one with consternation like the gasps of a dying man; indeed, it is just that. It enthralls us as whirlpools enthrall us, but at the same time it robs us of what was supposed to be said but was not said, thus frustrating and distancing us. I think that Celan the poet must be considered and mourned rather than imitated. If his is a message, it is lost in the 'background noise.' It is not communication; it is not a language, or at the most it is a dark and maimed language, precisely that of someone who is about to die and is alone, as we will all be at the moment of death" (Levi 1990: 637).

In Auschwitz, Levi had already attempted to listen to and interpret an inarticulate babble, something like a non-language or a dark and maimed language. It was in the days that followed the liberation of the camp, when the Russians moved the survivors from Buna to the "big camp" of Auschwitz. Here Levi's attention was immediately drawn to a child the deportees called Hurbinek:

> Hurbinek was a nobody, a child of death, a child of Auschwitz. He looked about three years old, no one knew anything of him, he could not speak and had no name; that curious name, Hurbinek, had been given to him by us, perhaps by one of the women who had interpreted with those syllables one of the inarticulate sounds that the baby let out now and again. He was paralyzed from the waist down, with atrophied legs, as thin as sticks; but his eyes, lost in his triangular and wasted face, flashed terribly alive, full of demand, assertion, of the will to break loose, to shatter the tomb of his dumbness. The speech he lacked, which no one had bothered to teach him, the need of speech charged his stare with explosive urgency (Levi 1986: 191).

37

Now at a certain point Hurbinek begins to repeat a word over and over again, a word that no one in the camp can understand and that Levi doubtfully transcribes as *mass-klo* or *matisklo*. "During the night we listened carefully: it was true, from Hurbinek's corner there occasionally came a sound, a word. It was not, admittedly, always exactly the same word, but it was certainly an articulated word; or better, several slightly different articulated words, experimental variations of a theme, on a root, perhaps even on a name" (Levi 1986: 192). They all listen and try to decipher that sound, that emerging vocabulary; but, despite the presence of all the languages of Europe in the camp, Hurbinek's word remains obstinately secret. "No, it was certainly not a message, it was not a revelation; perhaps it was his name, if it had ever fallen to his lot to be given a name; perhaps (according to one of our hypotheses) it meant 'to eat,' or 'bread'; or perhaps 'meat' in Bohemian, as one of us who knew that language maintained.... Hurbinek, the nameless, whose tiny forearm — even his — bore the tattoo of Auschwitz; Hurbinek died in the first days of March 1945, free but not redeemed. Nothing remains of him: he bears witness through these words of mine" (*ibid.*).

Perhaps this was the secret word that Levi discerned in the "background noise" of Celan's poetry. And yet in Auschwitz, Levi nevertheless attempted to listen to that to which no one has borne witness, to gather the secret word: *mass-klo*, *matisklo*. Perhaps every word, every writing is born, in this sense, as testimony. This is why what is borne witness to cannot already be language or writing. It can only be something to which no one has borne witness. And this is the sound that arises from the lacuna, the non-language that one speaks when one is alone, the non-language to which language answers, in which language is born. It is necessary to reflect on the nature of that to which no one has borne witness, on this non-language.

1.15   Hurbinek cannot bear witness, since he does not have language (the speech that he utters is a sound that is uncertain and meaningless: *mass-klo* or *matisklo*). And yet he "bears witness through these words of mine." But not even the survivor can bear witness completely, can speak his own lacuna. This means that testimony is the disjunction between two impossibilities of bearing witness; it means that language, in order to bear witness, must give way to a non-language in order to show the impossibility of bearing witness. The language of testimony is a language that no longer signifies and that, in not signifying, advances into what is without language, to the point of taking on a different insignificance — that of the complete witness, that of he who by definition cannot bear witness. To bear witness, it is therefore not enough to bring language to its own non-sense, to the pure undecidability of letters (*m-a-s-s-k-l-o*, *m-a-t-i-s-k-l-o*). It is necessary that this senseless sound be, in turn, the voice of something or someone that, for entirely other reasons, cannot bear witness. It is thus necessary that the impossibility of bearing witness, the "lacuna" that constitutes human language, collapses, giving way to a different impossibility of bearing witness — that which does not have language.

The trace of that to which no one has borne witness, which language believes itself to transcribe, is not the speech of language. The speech of language is born where language is no longer in the beginning, where language falls away from it simply to bear witness: "It was not light, but was sent to bear witness to the light."

39

CHAPTER TWO

The *Muselmann*

2.1   The untestifiable, that to which no one has borne witness, has a name. In the jargon of the camp, it is *der Muselmann*, literally "the Muslim."

> The so-called *Muselmann*, as the camp language termed the prisoner who was giving up and was given up by his comrades, no longer had room in his consciousness for the contrasts good or bad, noble or base, intellectual or unintellectual. He was a staggering corpse, a bundle of physical functions in its last convulsions. As hard as it may be for us to do so, we must exclude him from our considerations (Améry 1980: 9).

(Again the lacuna in testimony, one which is now consciously affirmed.)

> I remember that while we were going down the stairs leading to the baths, they had us accompanied by a group of *Muselmänner*, as we later called them — mummy-men, the living dead. They made them go down the stairs with us only to show them to us, as if to say, "you'll become like them" (Carpi 1993: 17).

41

The SS man was walking slowly, looking at the Muslim who was coming toward him. We looked to the left, to see what would happen. Dragging his wooden clogs, the dull-witted and aimless creature ended up bumping right into the SS officer, who yelled at him and gave him a lashing on the head. The Muslim stood still, without realizing what had happened. When he received a second and, then, a third lashing because he had forgotten to take off his cap, he began to do it on himself, as he had dysentery. When the SS man saw the black, stinking liquid begin to cover his clogs, he went crazy. He hurled himself on top of the Muslim and began kicking his stomach with all his strength. Even after the poor thing had fallen into his own excrement, the SS man kept beating his head and chest. The Muslim didn't defend himself. With the first kick, he folded in two, and after a few more he was dead (Ryn and Klodzinski 1987: 128–29).

Two phases must be distinguished in the symptoms of malnutrition. The first is characterized by weight loss, muscular asthenia, and progressive energy loss in movement. At this stage, the organism is not yet deeply damaged. Aside from the slowness of movement and the loss of strength, those suffering from malnutrition still do not show any symptoms. If one disregards a certain degree of excitability and irritability, not even psychological changes can be detected. It was difficult to recognize the point of passage into the second stage. In some cases it happened slowly and gradually; in others it happened very quickly. It was possible to ascertain that the second phase began when the starving individual lost a third of his normal weight. If he continued losing weight, his facial expression also changed. His gaze became cloudy and his face took on an indifferent, mechanical, sad expression. His eyes became covered by a kind of layer and seemed deeply set in his face. His skin took on a pale gray color, becoming thin and hard like paper. He became very sensitive to every kind of infection and contagion, especially scabies. His hair became bristly, opaque, and split easily. His head became longer, his cheek bones and eye sockets became more pronounced. He breathed slowly; he spoke softly and with great difficulty. Depending on how long he had been in this state of malnutrition, he suffered from small or large edemas. They appeared on his lower eyelids and his feet and, then, on other parts of his body depending on the time of day. In the morning, after his night-time sleep, they were most visible on his face. In the evening, on the other hand, they most easily could be seen on his feet and the lower and upper parts of his legs. Being on his feet all the time made all the liquids in him accumulate in the lower part of his body. As the state of malnutrition grew, the edemas multiplied, especially on those who had to stand on their feet for many hours — first on the lower part of their legs, then on their behinds and testicles and even on their abdomens. The swellings were often accompanied by diarrhea, which often preceded the development of edemas. In this phase, they became indifferent to everything happening around them. They excluded themselves from all relations to their environment. If they could still move around, they did so in slow motion, without bending their knees. They shivered since their body temperature usually fell below 98.7 degrees. Seeing them from afar, one had the impression of seeing Arabs praying. This image was the origin of the term used at Auschwitz for people dying of malnutrition: Muslims (*ibid.*: 94).

No one felt compassion for the Muslim, and no one felt sympathy for him either. The other inmates, who continually feared for their lives, did not even judge him worthy of being looked at. For the prisoners who collaborated, the Muslims were a source of anger and worry; for the SS, they were merely useless garbage. Every group thought only about eliminating them, each in its own way (*ibid.*: 127).

43

All the *Muselmänner* who finished in the gas chambers have the same story, or more exactly, have no story; they followed the slope down to the bottom, like streams that run down to the sea. On their entry into the camp, through basic incapacity, or by misfortune, or through some banal incident, they are overcome before they can adapt themselves; they are beaten by time, they do not begin to learn German, to disentangle the infernal knot of laws and prohibitions until their body is already in decay, and nothing can save them from selections or from death by exhaustion. Their life is short, but their number is endless; they, the *Muselmänner*, the drowned, form the backbone of the camp, an anonymous mass, continually renewed and always identical, of non-men who march and labour in silence, the divine spark dead in them, already too empty to really suffer. One hesitates to call them living: one hesitates to call their death death, in the face of which they have no fear, as they are too tired to understand.

They crowd my memory with their faceless presence, and if I could enclose all the evil of our time in one image, I would choose this image which is familiar to me: an emaciated man, with head dropped and shoulders curved, on whose face and in whose eyes not a trace of thought is to be seen (Levi 1986: 90).

2.2   There is little agreement on the origin of the term *Muselmann*. As is often the case with jargon, the term is not lacking in synonyms. "The expression was in common use especially in Auschwitz, from where it spread to other camps as well.... In Majdanek, the word was unknown. The living dead there were termed 'donkeys'; in Dachau they were 'cretins,' in Stutthof 'cripples,' in Mauthausen 'swimmers,' in Neuengamme 'camels,' in Buchenwald 'tired sheikhs,' and in the women's camp known as Ravensbrück, *Muselweiber* (female Muslims) or 'trinkets'"(Sofsky 1997: 329n5).

The most likely explanation of the term can be found in the literal meaning of the Arabic word muslim: the one who submits unconditionally to the will of God. It is this meaning that lies at the origin of the legends concerning Islam's supposed fatalism, legends which are found in European culture starting with the Middle Ages (this deprecatory sense of the term is present in European languages, particularly in Italian). But while the muslim's resignation consists in the conviction that the will of Allah is at work every moment and in even the smallest events, the *Muselmann* of Auschwitz is instead defined by a loss of all will and consciousness. Hence Kogon's statement that in the camps, the "relatively large group of men who had long since lost any real will to survive ... were called 'Moslems' — men of unconditional fatalism" (Kogon 1979: 284).

There are other, less convincing explanations. One example appears in the *Encyclopedia Judaica* under the entry *Muselmann*: "Used mainly at Auschwitz, the term appears to derive from the typical attitude of certain deportees, that is, staying crouched on the ground, legs bent in Oriental fashion, faces rigid as masks." Another explanation is suggested by Marsalek, who associates "the typical movements of *Muselmänner*, the swaying motions of the upper part of the body, with Islamic prayer rituals" (Sofsky 1997: 329n5). There is also the rather improbable interpretation of *Muselmann* as *Muschelmann*, "shell-man," a man folded and closed upon himself (Levi seems to allude to this interpretation when he writes of "husk-men").

In any case, it is certain that, with a kind of ferocious irony, the Jews knew that they would not die at Auschwitz as Jews.

2.3   This disagreement concerning the etymology of the term *Muselmann* has as its precise counterpart an uncertainty as to the semantic and disciplinary field in which the term should be

situated. It is not surprising that the physician Fejkiel, who worked
for a long time in the concentration camps, tended to treat the
Muselmann as a medical case, beset with a particular malnutri-
tional disorder endemic to the camps. To a certain degree, it was
Bruno Bettelheim who first considered this issue, when in 1943
he published his essay "Individual and Mass Behavior in Extreme
Situations" in the *Journal of Abnormal and Social Psychology*. In
1938–39, before being liberated, Bettelheim spent a year in Dachau
and Buchenwald, which at the time were the two largest Nazi concentration camps for political prisoners. Though the living conditions of the camps during those years cannot be compared to
Auschwitz, Bettelheim had seen *Muselmänner* with his own eyes,
and immediately recognized the novel transformations that "extreme situations" produced in the personalities of camp prisoners. For him, the *Muselmann* became the paradigm through which
he conceived his study of childhood schizophrenia, written years
after he immigrated to the United States. The Orthogenic School,
which he founded in Chicago to treat autistic children, thus had
the form of a kind of counter-camp, in which he undertook to
teach *Muselmänner* to become men again. There is not one character trait in Bettelheim's detailed phenomenology of childhood
autism described in *The Empty Fortress* that does not have its
dark precursor and interpretative paradigm in the behavior of the
Muselmann. "What was external reality for the prisoner is for the
autistic child his inner reality. Each ends up, though for different
reasons, with a parallel experience of the world" (Bettelheim
1967: 65). Just as autistic children totally ignored reality in order
to retreat into an imaginary world, so the prisoners who became
Muselmänner substituted delirious fantasies for the relations of
causality to which they no longer paid any attention. In the semi-
cross-eyed gaze, hesitant walk, and stubborn repetitiveness and
silence of Joey, Marcie, Laurie, and the other children of the

school, Bettelheim sought a possible solution to the enigma that the *Muselmann* had confronted him with at Dachau. Nevertheless, for Bettelheim, the concept of "extreme situation" continued to imply a moral and political connotation; for him, the *Muselmann* could never be reduced to a clinical category. Because what was at stake in the extreme situation was "to remain alive and unchanged as a person" (Bettelheim 1960: 158), the *Muselmann* in some sense marked the moving threshold in which man passed into non-man and in which clinical diagnosis passed into anthropological analysis.

As for Levi, whose first testimony was a "Report on the Hygenic and Sanitary Organization of the Monowitz (Auschwitz, High Silesia) Concentration Camp for Jews," written in 1946 at the request of the Soviet authorities, the nature of the experience to which he was called to bear witness was never in question. "Actually, what interests me is the dignity and lack of dignity of man," he declared in 1986 to Barbara Kleiner, with a sense of irony that probably went unnoticed by his interviewer (Levi 1997: 78). The new ethical material that he discovered at Auschwitz allowed for neither summary judgments nor distinctions and, whether he liked it or not, lack of dignity had to interest him as much as dignity. As suggested by the ironically rhetorical Italian title *Se questo è un uomo* (literally "If This Is a Man," translated as *Survival in Auschwitz* in English), in Auschwitz ethics begins precisely at the point where the *Muselmann*, the "complete witness," makes it forever impossible to distinguish between man and non-man.

An explicit political meaning has also been attributed to the extreme threshold between life and death, the human and the inhuman, that the *Muselmann* inhabits:

The *Muselmann* embodies the anthropological meaning of absolute power in an especially radical form. Power abrogates itself in the act of killing. The death of the other puts an end to the social relationship. But by starving the other, it gains time. It erects a third realm, a limbo between life and death. Like the pile of corpses, the *Muselmänner* document the total triumph of power over the human being. Although still nominally alive, they are nameless hulks. In the configuration of their infirmity, as in organized mass murder, the regime realizes its quintessential self (Sofsky 1997: 294).

At times a medical figure or an ethical category, at times a political limit or an anthropological concept, the *Muselmann* is an indefinite being in whom not only humanity and non-humanity, but also vegetative existence and relation, physiology and ethics, medicine and politics, and life and death continuously pass through each other. This is why the *Muselmann*'s "third realm" is the perfect cipher of the camp, the non-place in which all disciplinary barriers are destroyed and all embankments flooded.

2.4   Recently, philosophers and theologians alike have invoked the paradigm of the "extreme situation" or "limit situation." The function of this paradigm is analogous to the function ascribed by some jurists to the state of exception. Just as the state of exception allows for the foundation and definition of the normal legal order, so in the light of the extreme situation — which is, at bottom, a kind of exception — it is possible to judge and decide on the normal situation. As Kierkegaard writes, "the exception explains the general as well as itself. And when one really wants to study the general, one need only look around for a real exception." In Bettelheim, the camp, as the exemplary extreme situation, thus allows for the determination of what is inhuman and human and, in this way, for the separation of the *Muselmann* from the human being.

Referring to the concept of the limit situation and, in particular, to the experience of the Second World War, Karl Barth justly

observed that human beings have the striking capacity to adapt
so well to an extreme situation that it can no longer function as
a distinguishing criterion. "According to the present trend," he
wrote in 1948,

> we may suppose that even on the morning after the Day of Judg-
> ment — if such a thing were possible — every cabaret, every night
> club, every newspaper firm eager for advertisements and subscribers,
> every nest of political fanatics, every discussion group, indeed, every
> Christian tea-party and Church synod would resume business to the
> best of its ability, and with a new sense of opportunity, completely
> unmoved, quite uninstructed, and in no serious sense different from
> what it was before. Fire, drought, earthquake, war, pestilence, the
> darkening of the sun and similar phenomena are not the things to
> plunge us into real anguish, and therefore to give us real peace. "The
> Lord was not in the storm, the earthquake or the fire" (1 Kings 19:
> 11ff.). He really was not (Barth 1960: 115).

All the witnesses, even those submitted to the most extreme
conditions (for example, the members of the *Sonderkommando*),
recall the incredible tendency of the limit situation to become
habit ("doing this work, one either goes crazy the first day or
gets used to it"). The Nazis so well understood this secret power
inherent in every limit situation that they never revoked the state
of exception declared in February 1933, upon their rise to power.
In this sense, the Third Reich has been aptly defined as a "Night
of St. Bartholomew that lasted twelve years."

Auschwitz is precisely the place in which the state of exception coincides perfectly with the rule and the extreme situation
becomes the very paradigm of daily life. But it is this paradoxical
tendency of the limit situation to turn over into its opposite that
makes it interesting. As long as the state of exception and the

normal situation are kept separate in space and time, as is usually the case, both remain opaque, though they secretly institute each other. But as soon as they show their complicity, as happens more and more often today, they illuminate each other, so to speak, from the inside. And yet this implies that the extreme situation can no longer function as a distinguishing criterion, as it did for Bettelheim; it implies that the extreme situation's lesson is rather that of absolute immanence, of "everything being in everything." In this sense, philosophy can be defined as the world seen from an extreme situation that has become the rule (according to some philosophers, the name of this extreme situation is "God").

2.5   Aldo Carpi, professor of painting at the Academy of Brera, was deported to Gusen in February 1944, where he remained until May 1945. He managed to survive because the SS began to commission paintings and drawings from him once they discovered his profession. They mostly commissioned family portraits, which Carpi produced from photographs; but there were also requests for Italian landscapes and "Venetian nudes," which Carpi painted from memory. Carpi was not a realistic painter, and yet one can understand why he wanted to paint the actual scenes and figures from the camp. But his commissioners had absolutely no interest in such things; indeed, they did not even tolerate the sight of them. "No one wants camp scenes and figures," Carpi notes in his diary, "no one wants to see the *Muselmann*" (Carpi 1993: 33).

Other witnesses confirm this impossibility of gazing upon the *Muselmann*. One account is particularly eloquent, even if it is indirect. A few years ago, the English film shot in Bergen-Belsen immediately after the camp's liberation in 1945 was made available to the public. It is difficult to bear the sight of the thousands of naked corpses piled in common graves or carried on the shoulders of former camp guards, of those tortured bodies that even the SS could not name (we know from witnesses that under no circumstances were they to be called "corpses" or "cadavers," but rather simply *Figuren*, figures, dolls). And yet since the Allies intended to use this footage as proof of Nazi atrocities and make it public in Germany, we are spared no detail of the terrible spectacle. At one point, however, the camera lingers almost by accident on what seem to be living people, a group of prisoners crouched on the ground or wandering on foot like ghosts. It lasts only a few seconds, but it is still long enough for the spectator to realize that they are either *Muselmänner* who have survived by some miracle or, at least, prisoners very close to the state of *Muselmänner*. With the exception of Carpi's drawings, which he did from memory, this is perhaps the sole image of *Muselmänner* we have. Nevertheless, the same cameraman who had until then patiently lingered over naked bodies, over the terrible "dolls" dismembered and stacked one on top of another, could not bear the sight of these half-living beings; he immediately began once again to show the cadavers. As Elias Canetti has noted, a heap of dead bodies is an ancient spectacle, one which has often satisfied the powerful. But the sight of *Muselmänner* is an absolutely new phenomenon, unbearable to human eyes.

2.6   What no one wants to see at any cost, however, is the "core" of the camp, the fatal threshold that all prisoners are constantly about to cross. "The *Muselmann* stage was the great fear of the prisoners, since not one of them knew when his fate would become that of the Muslim, the sure candidate for the gas chambers or another kind of death" (Langbein 1972: 113).

The space of the camp (at least of those camps, like Auschwitz, in which concentration camp and extermination camp coincide) can even be represented as a series of concentric circles that, like waves, incessantly wash up against a central non-place, where the *Muselmann* lives. In camp jargon, the extreme limit of this non-place is called *Selektion*, the selection procedure for the gas chamber. This is why the prisoner's most pressing concern was to hide his sickness and his exhaustion, to constantly cover over the *Muselmann* who at every moment was emerging in him. The entire population of the camp is, indeed, nothing other than an immense whirlpool obsessively spinning around a faceless center. But like the mystical rose of Dante's *Paradiso*, this anonymous vortex is "painted in our image" (*pinta della nostra effige*); it bears the true likeness of man. According to the law that what man despises is also what he fears resembles him, the *Muselmann* is universally avoided because everyone in the camp recognizes himself in his disfigured face.

It is a striking fact that although all witnesses speak of him as a central experience, the *Muselmann* is barely named in the historical studies on the destruction of European Jewry. Perhaps only now, almost fifty years later, is the *Muselmann* becoming visible; perhaps only now may we draw the consequences of this visibility. For this visibility implies that the paradigm of extermination, which has until now exclusively oriented interpretations of the concentration camp, is not replaced by, but rather accompanied by, another paradigm, a paradigm that casts new light on the extermination itself, making it in some way even more atrocious. Before being a death camp, Auschwitz is the site of an experiment that remains unthought today, an experiment beyond life and death in which the Jew is transformed into a *Muselmann* and the human being into a non-human. And we will not understand what Auschwitz is if we do not first understand who or what the *Muselmann* is — if we do not learn to gaze with him upon the Gorgon.

2.7   One of the paraphrases by which Levi designates the *Musel-mann* is "he who has seen the Gorgon." But what has the *Musel-mann* seen, and what, in the camp, is the Gorgon?

In an exemplary study that draws on literature, sculpture, and vase painting, François Frontisi-Ducroux has shown how the Greeks conceived of the Gorgon, that horrid female head covered with serpents whose gaze produced death and which Perseus, with Athena's help, had to cut off without seeing.

First of all, the Gorgon does not have a face in the sense ex-pressed by the Greek term *prosopon*, which etymologically signi-fies "what stands before the eyes, what gives itself to be seen." The prohibited face, which cannot be seen because it produces death, is for the Greeks a non-face and as such is never designated by the term *prosopon*. Yet for the Greeks this impossible vision is at the same time absolutely inevitable. Not only is the Gorgon's non-face represented innumerable times in sculpture and vase painting; the most curious fact concerns the mode of the Gor-gon's presentation. "Gorgo, the 'anti-face,' is represented only through a face...in an ineluctable confrontation of gazes...this *antiprosopon* is given over to the gaze in its fullness, with a clear demonstration of the signs of her dangerous visual effects" (Fron-tisi-Ducroux 1995: 68). Breaking with the iconographical tradi-tion by which the human figure is drawn in vase painting only in profile, the Gorgon does not have a profile; she is always pre-sented as a flat plate, without a third dimension — that is, not as a real face but as an absolute image, as something that can only be seen and presented. The *gorgoneion*, which represents the impos-sibility of vision, is what cannot *not* be seen.

But there is more. Frontisi-Ducroux establishes a parallel be-tween this frontality, which breaks with the iconographical con-vention of vase painting, and apostrophe, the rhetorical figure by which the author, rupturing narrative convention, turns to a

53

character or directly to the public. This means that the impossibility of vision of which the Gorgon is the cipher contains something like an apostrophe, a call that cannot be avoided.

But then "he who has seen the Gorgon" cannot be a simple designation for the *Muselmann*. If to see the Gorgon means to see the impossibility of seeing, then the Gorgon does not name something that exists or that happens in the camp, something that the *Muselmann*, and not the survivor, would have seen. Rather, the Gorgon designates the impossibility of seeing that belongs to the camp inhabitant, the one who has "touched bottom" in the camp and has become a non-human. The *Muselmann* has neither seen nor known anything, if not the impossibility of knowing and seeing. This is why to bear witness to the *Muselmann*, to attempt to contemplate the impossibility of seeing, is not an easy task.

That at the "bottom" of the human being there is nothing other than an impossibility of seeing — this is the Gorgon, whose vision transforms the human being into a non-human. That precisely this inhuman impossibility of seeing is what calls and addresses the human, the apostrophe from which human beings cannot turn away — this and nothing else is testimony. The Gorgon and he who has seen her and the *Muselmann* and he who bears witness to him are one gaze; they are a single impossibility of seeing.

2.8   That one cannot truly speak of "living beings" when referring to *Muselmänner* is confirmed by all the witnesses. Améry and Bettelheim define them as "walking corpses" (Améry 1980: 9, Bettelheim 1979: 106). Carpi calls them "living dead" and "mummy-men" (Carpi 1993: 17); "one hesitates to call them living," writes Levi (1986: 90). "Finally, you confuse the living and the dead," writes a witness of Bergen-Belsen. "Basically, the difference is minimal anyhow. We're skeletons that are still moving; and they're skeletons that are already immobile. But there's even

54

a third category: the ones who lie stretched out, unable to move, but still breathing slightly" (Sofsky 1997: 328n2). "Faceless presences" or "shadows," in every case they inhabit "the limit between life and death" — to cite the title of Ryn's and Klodzinski's study dedicated to the *Muselmann*, which today remains the sole monograph on the subject.

But this biological image is immediately accompanied by another image, which by contrast seems to contain the true sense of the matter. The *Muselmann* is not only or not so much a limit between life and death; rather, he marks the threshold between the human and the inhuman.

The witnesses are in agreement about this too. "Non-men who march and labor in silence, the divine spark dead within them" (Levi 1986: 90). "They had to give up responding to it [the environment] at all, and become objects, but with this they gave up being persons" (Bettelheim 1960: 152). There is thus a point at which human beings, while apparently remaining human beings, cease to be human. This point is the *Muselmann*, and the camp is his exemplary site. But what does it mean for a human being to become a non-human? Is there a humanity of human beings that can be distinguished and separated from human beings' biological humanity?

2.9   What is at stake in the "extreme situation" is, therefore, "remaining a human being or not," becoming a *Muselmann* or not. The most immediate and common impulse is to interpret this limit experience in moral terms. It was thus a question of trying to preserve dignity and self-respect, even if in the camp dignity and respect could not always be translated into corresponding actions. Bettelheim seems to imply something of the kind when he speaks of a "point of no return" beyond which the prisoner became a *Muselmann*:

To survive as a man not as a walking corpse, as a debased and degraded but still human being, one had first and foremost to remain informed and aware of what made up one's personal point of no return, the point beyond which one would never, under any circumstances, give in to the oppressor, even if it meant risking and losing one's life. It meant being aware that if one survived at the price of overreaching this point one would be holding on to a life that had lost all its meaning. It would mean surviving — not with a lowered self-respect, but without any (Bettelheim 1960: 157).

Naturally, Bettelheim realized that in the extreme situation, real freedom and choice were practically non-existent and often amounted to the degree of inner awareness with which one obeyed an order:

This keeping informed and aware of one's actions — though it could not alter the required act, save in extremities — this minimal distance from one's own behavior, and the freedom to feel differently about it depending on its character, this too was what permitted the prisoner to remain a human being. It was the giving up of all feelings, all inner reservations about one's actions, the letting go of a point at which one would hold fast no matter what, that changed prisoner into moslem.... Prisoners who understood this fully, came to know that this, and only this, formed the crucial difference between retaining one's humanity (and often life itself) and accepting death as a human being (or perhaps physical death) (Bettelheim 1960: 158).

For Bettelheim, the *Muselmann* is therefore the one who has abdicated his inalienable freedom and has consequently lost all traces of affective life and humanity. This passage beyond the "point of no return" is such a disturbing experience and, for

Bettelheim, becomes such a criterion of moral distinction between human and non-human as to deprive the witness not only
of all pity, but also of lucidity, bringing him to mistake what ought
never to be confused. Thus Höss, the commander of Auschwitz
condemned in Poland in 1947, is transformed for Bettelheim into
a kind of "well fed and well clothed" *Muselmann*.

> While his physical death came later, he became a living corpse from
> the time he assumed command of Auschwitz. That he never became
> a "moslem" was because he continued to be well fed and well
> clothed. But he had to divest himself so entirely of self respect and
> self love, of feeling and personality, that for all practical purposes he
> was little more than a machine functioning only as his superiors
> flicked the buttons of command (Bettelheim 1960: 238).

To his eyes, the *Muselmann* also becomes an improbable and
monstrous biological machine, lacking not only all moral conscience, but even sensibility and nervous stimuli. "One might even
speculate," Bettelheim writes,

> as to whether these organisms had by-passed the reflex arc that once
> extended from external or internal stimulus via frontal lobes to feel-
> ing and action.... Prisoners entered the moslem stage when emo-
> tion could no longer be evoked in them.... Despite their hunger,
> even the food stimulus reached their brain clearly enough to lead to
> action.... Other prisoners often tried to be nice to them when they
> could, to give them food and so forth, but they could no longer
> respond to the emotional attitude that was behind someone's giving
> them food (Bettelheim 1960: 152, 156).

Here the principle according to which "no one wants to see
the *Muselmann*" involves the survivor as well. Not only does he

falsify his own testimony (all the witnesses agree that no one in the camps "was good to the *Muselmänner*"), he does not realize that he has transformed human beings into an unreal paradigm, a vegetative machine. The sole goal of this paradigm is to allow at any cost for the distinction of what, in the camps, has become indistinguishable: the human and the inhuman.

2.10   What does it mean "to remain human"? That the answer is not easy and the question itself needs to be considered is implicit in the survivor's warning: "Consider if this is a man." At issue is not a question, but an injunction ("I command these words to you" [Levi 1986: 11]) that calls into question the very form of the question — as if the last thing one can expect here is a statement or a denial.

Instead, it is necessary to withdraw the meaning of the term "man" to the point at which the very sense of the question is transformed. It is remarkable that Levi's and Antelme's testimonies, which were both published in 1947, seem to engage in an ironic dialogue on this subject even in their titles, *If This Is a Man* and *The Human Species*. For Antelme, at issue in the camps was an "almost biological" claim to belong to the human species, the final sentiment of belonging to a species: "the negation of our quality as men provokes an almost biological claim of belonging to the human species [*espèce*]" (Antelme 1992: 5–6, translation slightly emended).

It is important that Antelme uses the technical term *espèce* here instead of referring to the more familiar one of *le genre humain*. For it is a matter of biological belonging in the strict sense (the "almost" is a euphemism of sorts, a slight scruple before the unimagined), not of a declaration of moral or political solidarity. And precisely this is what must be "considered," and considered not as a question of dignity, as Bettelheim seems to think. The task is so dark and enormous as to coincide with the one set by the SS: to take seriously the law of the camp, "pigs, not men."

> Of the heroes we know about, from history or from literature, whether it was love they cried forth, or solitude, or vengeance, or the anguish of being or of non-being, whether it was humiliation they rose up against, or injustice — of these heroes we do not believe that they were ever able to express as their last and only claim an ultimate sense of belonging to the human race. To say that one felt oneself contested as a man, as a member of the human species — may look like a feeling discovered in retrospect, an explanation arrived at afterwards. And yet it was that we felt most constantly and immediately, and that — exactly that — was what the others wanted (*ibid.*: translation slightly emended).

What is the "ultimate" sense of belonging to the human species? And does such a sense exist? For many, the *Muselmann* seems to constitute nothing other than an answer to this question.

2.11 Levi begins to bear witness only after dehumanization has been achieved, only once it no longer makes any sense to speak of dignity. He is the only one who consciously sets out to bear witness in place of the *Muselmänner*, the drowned, those who were demolished and who touched bottom. It is implicit in many testimonies that at Auschwitz everyone somehow set their human dignity aside. But perhaps nowhere is this expressed as clearly as in the passage in *The Drowned and the Saved* in which Levi evokes the strange desperation that overcame the prisoners at the moment of liberation: "Just as they felt they were again becoming men, that is, responsible..." (Levi 1989: 70). The survivor is therefore familiar with the common necessity of degradation; he knows that humanity and responsibility are something that the deportee had to abandon when entering the camp.

It is important that certain individuals — pious Chaim, taciturn Szabo, sage Robert, courageous Baruch — did not give in. But testimony is not for them; it is not for the "better ones." And even if they had not died — but "the best all died" (*ibid.*: 82) — they would not be the witnesses; they would not be able to bear witness to the camp. Perhaps to something else — their own faith, their own strength (and this is precisely what they did, in dying) — but not to the camp. The "complete witnesses," those for whom bearing witness makes sense, "had already lost the ability to observe, to remember, to compare and express themselves" (*ibid.*: 84). To speak of dignity and decency in their case would not be decent.

When one of his friends tried to convince him that his survival was providential, that he had been "marked, chosen," Levi responds with contempt — "Such an opinion seemed monstrous to me" (*ibid.*: 82). Levi suggests that to claim that a recognizable good was kept at Auschwitz, that something precious was in the camp and carried out into the normal world, is not acceptable and does not bear witness to the good. This too is the meaning of the thesis that it is not the "best, those predestined to do good, the bearers of a message" who survive (*ibid.*: 82). The survivors are not only "worse" in comparison with the best ones — those whose strength rendered them less fit in the camp — they are also "worse" in comparison with the anonymous mass of the drowned, those whose death cannot be called death. This is the specific ethical aporia of Auschwitz: it is the site in which it is not decent to remain decent, in which those who believed themselves to preserve their dignity and self-respect experience shame with respect to those who did not.

2.12   In *The Notebooks of Malte Laurids Brigge*, Rilke provides a famous description of the shame that comes from having preserved decency and dignity. Encountering some vagrants in the streets of Paris, Malte recognizes that, despite his apparent dignity and clean collar, the vagrants identify him as one of them:

True, my collar is clean, my underwear too, and I could, just as I am, walk into any café I felt like, possibly even on the grand boulevards, and confidently reach out my hand to a plate full of pastries and help myself. No one would find that surprising; no one would shout at me or throw me out, for it is after all a genteel hand, a hand that is washed four or five times a day.... Though there are still one or two individuals, on the Boulevard Saint-Michel for example, or on the rue Racine, who are not fooled, who don't give a damn about my wrists. They look at me and know. They know that in reality I am one of them, that I'm only acting.... And they don't want to spoil my fun; they just grin a little and wink at me.... Who are these people? What do they want of me? Are they waiting for me? How do they recognize me?... For it's obvious they are outcasts, not just beggars; no, they are really not beggars, there is a difference. They are human trash, husks of men that fate has spewed out. Wet with the spittle of fate, they stick to a wall, a lamp-post, a billboard, or they trickle slowly down the street, leaving a dark, filthy trail behind them.... And how did that small, gray woman come to be standing at my side for a whole quarter of an hour in front of a store window, showing me an old, long pencil that pushed infinitely slowly up out of her wretched, clenched hands. I pretended that I was busy looking at the display in the window and hadn't noticed a thing. But she knew I had seen her; she knew I was standing there trying to figure out what she was doing. For I understood quite well that the pencil in itself was of no importance: I felt that it was a sign, a sign for the initiated, a sign only outcasts could recognize; I sensed that she was directing me to go somewhere or do something. And the strangest part was that I couldn't get rid of the feeling that there actually existed some kind of secret language which this sign belonged to, and that this scene was after all something that I should have expected.... Since then, hardly a day has passed without a similar encounter. Not only in the twilight, but at noon, in the busiest streets, a little man or an old woman will suddenly appear, nod to me, show me something, and then vanish, as if everything necessary were now done. It is possible that one fine day they will decide to come as far as my room; they certainly know where I live, and they'll manage to get past the concierge (Rilke 1983: 38–41).

What interests us here is less that Malte expresses the fundamental ambiguity of Rilke's gesture, which is divided between the consciousness of having abandoned every recognizable human aspect and of attempting to elude this situation at any cost, and by which every descent into the abyss becomes merely a preface to the predictable ascent into the *hauts lieux* of poetry and nobility. What is decisive, rather, is that when confronted with the outcasts, Malte realizes that his dignity is a useless comedy, something that can only induce them to "grin a little and wink" at him. The sight of them, the intimacy they suggest, is so unbearable to Malte that he fears they may one day appear at his house to bring shame upon him. This is why he takes refuge in the *Bibliothèque Nationale*, among his fellow poets, where the outcasts will never be admitted.

Perhaps never before Auschwitz was the shipwreck of dignity in the face of an extreme figure of the human and the uselessness of self-respect before absolute degradation so effectively described. A subtle thread ties Malte's "husks of men" to the "husk-men" of whom Levi speaks. The young poet's small shame before the vagrants of Paris resembles a meek messenger who announces the great, unprecedented shame of the survivors in the face of the drowned.

2.13   The paradoxical ethical situation of the *Muselmann* must be considered. He is not so much, as Bettelheim believes, the cipher of the point of no return and the threshold beyond which one ceases to be human. He does not merely embody a moral death against which one must resist with all one's strength, to save humanity, self-respect, and perhaps even life. Rather, the *Muselmann*, as Levi describes him, is the site of an experiment in which morality and humanity themselves are called into question. The *Muselmann* is a limit figure of a special kind, in which not only categories such as dignity and respect but even the very idea of an ethical limit lose their meaning.

If one establishes a limit beyond which one ceases to be human, and all or most of humankind passes beyond it, this proves not the inhumanity of human beings but, instead, the insufficiency and abstraction of the limit. Imagine that the SS let a preacher enter the camp, and that he tried with every possible means to convince the *Muselmänner* of the necessity of keeping their dignity and self-respect even at Auschwitz. The preacher's gesture would be odious; his sermon would be an atrocious jest in the face of those who were beyond not only the possibility of per- suasion, but even of all human help ("they were nearly always beyond help" [Bettelheim 1960: 156]). This is why the prisoners have always given up speaking to the *Muselmann*, almost as if silence and not seeing were the only demeanor adequate for those who are beyond help.

Simply to deny the *Muselmann*'s humanity would be to accept the verdict of the SS and to repeat their gesture. The *Muselmann* has, instead, moved into a zone of the human where not only help but also dignity and self-respect have become useless. But if there is a zone of the human in which these concepts make no sense, then they are not genuine ethical concepts, for no ethics can claim to exclude a part of humanity, no matter how unpleasant or difficult that humanity is to see.

2.14   Years ago, a doctrine emerged that claimed to have identified a kind of transcendental condition of ethics in the form of a principle of obligatory communication. It originated in a European country that more than any other had reasons to have a guilty conscience with respect to Auschwitz, and it soon spread throughout academic circles. According to this curious doctrine, a speaking being cannot in any way avoid communication. Insofar as, unlike animals, they are gifted with language, human beings find themselves, so to speak, condemned to agree on the criteria of meaning and the validity of their actions. Whoever declares himself not wanting to communicate contradicts himself, for he has already communicated his will not to communicate.

Arguments of this kind are not new in the history of philosophy. They mark the point at which the philosopher finds himself at a loss, feeling the familiar ground of language somehow giving way beneath him. In his proof of the "strongest of all principles," the principle of non-contradiction, in Book Gamma of the *Metaphysics*, Aristotle is already compelled to take recourse to such argumentation. "Some, owing to a lack of training," he writes, "actually ask that it be demonstrated; for it is lack of training not to recognize of which things demonstration ought to be sought, and of which not. In general, it is impossible that there should be a demonstration of everything, since it would go on to infinity and, therefore, not be a demonstration.... But even this [the principle of non-contradiction] can be demonstrated, in the manner of a refutation, if only the disputant says something. If he says nothing, it is ridiculous to look for a statement in response to someone who says nothing; such a person, insofar as he is such, is altogether similar to a vegetable" (Aristotle 1993: 8, translation emended).

Insofar as they are founded on a tacit presupposition (in this case, that someone must speak), all refutations necessarily leave a residue in the form of an exclusion. In Aristotle, the residue is the plant-man, the man who does not speak. It suffices for the adversary simply and radically to cease speaking for the refutation to lose its force. Not that the entry into language is something that human beings can call into question as they see fit. Rather, the simple acquisition of speech in no way obliges one to speak. The pure pre-existence of language as the instrument of communication — the fact that, for speaking beings, language already exists — in itself contains no obligation to communicate. On the contrary, only if language is not always already communication, only if language bears witness to something to which it is impossible to bear witness, can a speaking being experience something like a necessity to speak.

Auschwitz is the radical refutation of every principle of obligatory communication. This is so not only because, according to survivors' testimonies, any attempt to induce a Kapo or an SS to communicate often ended in a beating; nor is it the case simply because, as Marsalek recalls, in certain camps the place of communication was taken by the rubber whip, ironically renamed *der Dolmetscher*, "the interpreter." Nor because "not being talked to" was the normal condition in the camp, where "your tongue dries up in a few days, and your thought with it" (Levi 1989: 93).

The decisive objection is different. It is, once again, the *Muselmann*. Let us imagine for a moment that a wondrous time machine places Professor Apel inside the camp. Placing a *Muselmann* before him, we ask him to verify his ethics of communication here too. At this point, it is best, in every possible way, to turn off our time machine and not continue the experiment. Despite all good intentions, the *Muselmann* risks once again being excluded from the human. The *Muselmann* is the radical refutation of every possible refutation, the destruction of those extreme metaphysical bulwarks whose force remains because they cannot be proven directly, but only by negating their negation.

2.15   It is not surprising that the concept of dignity also has a juridical origin. This time, however, the concept refers to the sphere of public law. Already in the Republican era, the Latin term *dignitas* indicates the rank and authority that inhere in public duties as well as, by extension, those duties themselves. It is thus possible to speak of *dignitas equestre, regia, imperatoria*. From this perspective, a reading of the twelfth book of the *Codex Iustinianus*, entitled *De Dignitatibus*, is particularly instructive. Its task is to assure full respect for the orders of the various "dignities" (not only the traditional ones of the senators and consuls, but also those of the prefect to the praetorian, of the provost to the sacred cubiculum, of the casket masters, decans, epidemetics, the metats, and the other degrees of Byzantine bureaucracy). It takes care to forbid access to duties (*porta dignitatis*) for those whose lives did not correspond to an appropriate rank (for example, those marked by public censorship or infamy). But the construction of a genuine theory of dignities is the work of medieval jurists and canonists. In a now classic book entitled *The King's Two Bodies: A Study in Mediaeval Political Theology*, Ernst Kantorowicz showed how legal science is strictly bound to theology in the formulation of one of the cardinal points of the theory of sovereignty: the perpetual character of political power. Dignity is emancipated from its bearer and becomes a fictitious person, a kind of mystical body that accompanies the royal body of the magistrate or the emperor, just as Christ's divine person doubles his human body. This emancipation culminates in the principle so

66

often repeated by medieval jurists that "dignity never dies" (*dignitas non moritur, Le Roi ne meurt jamais*).

The simultaneous separation and unity of dignity and its bodily bearer finds clear expression in the double funeral of the Roman Emperor (and, later, in that of the kings of France). Here a wax image of the dead sovereign, which represented his "dignity," is treated as a real person, receives honors and medical attention, and is burned in a solemn funeral rite (*funus imaginarium*).

The work of the canonists develops along lines parallel to those of the jurists. They construct a corresponding theory of the various ecclesiastical "dignities" that culminates in the *De dignitate sacerdotum* treatises used by officiates. On the one hand, the priest's rank is elevated beyond that of angels, insofar as during the mass, his body becomes the place of Christ's incarnation. On other hand, however, the ethics of dignity is emphasized, that is, the need for the priest to behave as befits his lofty position (thus to abstain from *mala vita*, for example, and not to handle the body of Christ after having touched female pudenda). And just as public dignity survives death in the form of an image, so priestly sanctity survives through the relic ("dignity" is the name that, above all in France, indicates the relics of the holy body).

When the term "dignity" is introduced into treatises of moral philosophy, the model developed by legal theory is simply followed, point by point, in order to be interiorized. In Rome as in the Middle Ages, the rank of the magistrate or priest is accompanied by a particular bearing and external appearance (from the beginning, *dignitas* also indicates the physical appearance adequate to an elevated condition and, according to the Romans, corresponds in man to feminine *venustas*). A pale image of dignity is thus spiritualized by moral philosophy and, then, usurps the place and name of the missing "dignity." And just as law once emancipated the rank of the *persona ficta* from its bearer, so

67

morality — with an inverse and specular gesture — liberates the bearing of the individual from the possession of a duty. A "dignified" person is now a person who, while lacking a public dignity, behaves in all matters as if he had one. This is clear in those classes which, after the fall of the ancien régime, lose even the last public prerogatives that absolute monarchy had given them. And, later, it can be observed in the lower classes, which are by definition excluded from every political dignity and to which all kinds of educators begin to teach lessons on the dignity and honesty of the poor. Both classes are compelled to live up to an absent dignity. The correspondence is often even linguistic: *dignitatem amittere* or *servare*, which indicated the loss or continuation of a duty, now becomes "to lose" or "to keep" dignity, to sacrifice or save, if not rank, then at least its appearance.

When referring to the legal status of Jews after the racial laws, the Nazis also used a term that implied a kind of dignity: *entwürdigen*, literally to "deprive of dignity." The Jew is a human being who has been deprived of all *Würde*, all dignity: he is merely human — and, for this reason, non-human.

2.16   In certain places and situations, dignity is out of place. The lover, for example, can be anything except "dignified," just as it is impossible to make love while keeping one's dignity. The ancients were so convinced of this impossibility that they maintained that even the name of amorous pleasure was incompatible with dignity (*verbum ipsum voluptatis non habet dignitatem*), and they classified erotic matters under the comic genre. (Servius informs us that Book Four of the *Aeneid*, which brings tears to the eyes of modern readers, was considered a perfect example of the comic style.)

There are good reasons for this impossibility of reconciling love and dignity. Both in the case of legal *dignitas* and in its moral transposition, dignity is something autonomous with respect to the existence of its bearer, an interior model or an external image to which he must conform and which must be preserved at all costs. But in extreme situations — and love, in its own way, is also an extreme situation — it is not possible to maintain even the slightest distance between real person and model, between life and norm. And this is not because life or the norm, the internal or the external, in turn takes the upper hand. It is rather because they are inseparable at every point, because they no longer leave any space for a dignified compromise. (St. Paul knows this perfectly when, in the Letter to the Romans, he defines love as the end and fulfillment of the Law.)

This is also why Auschwitz marks the end and the ruin of every ethics of dignity and conformity to a norm. The bare life to which human beings were reduced neither demands nor conforms to anything. It itself is the only norm; it is absolutely immanent. And "the ultimate sentiment of belonging to the species" cannot in any sense be a kind of dignity.

The good that the survivors were able to save from the camp — if there is any sense in speaking of a "good" here — is therefore not dignity. On the contrary, the atrocious news that the survivors carry from the camp to the land of human beings is precisely that it is possible to lose dignity and decency beyond imagination, that there is still life in the most extreme degradation. And this new knowledge now becomes the touchstone by which to judge and measure all morality and all dignity. The *Muselmann*, who is its most extreme expression, is the guard on the threshold of a new ethics, an ethics of a form of life that begins where dignity ends. And Levi, who bears witness to the drowned, speaking in their stead, is the cartographer of this new *terra ethica*, the implacable land-surveyor of *Muselmannland*.

2.17   We have seen that to be between life and death is one of the traits constantly attributed to the *Muselmann*, the "walking corpse" par excellence. Confronted with his disfigured face, his "Oriental" agony, the survivors hesitate to attribute to him even the mere dignity of the living. But this proximity to death may also have another, more appalling meaning, one which concerns the dignity or indignity of death rather than of life.

As always, it is Levi who finds the most just and, at the same time, most terrible formula: "One hesitates," he writes, "to call their death death." It is the most just formula, for what defines *Muselmänner* is not so much that their life is no longer life (this kind of degradation holds in a certain sense for all camp inhabitants and is not an entirely new experience) but, rather, that their death is not death. This — that the death of a human being can no longer be called death (not simply that it does not have importance, which is not new, but that it cannot be called by the name "death") — is the particular horror that the *Muselmann* brings to the camp and that the camp brings to the world. But this means — and this is why Levi's phrase is terrible — that the SS were right to call the corpses *Figuren*. Where death cannot be called death, corpses cannot be called corpses.

2.18   It has already been observed that what defines the camp is not simply the negation of life, that neither death nor the number of victims in any way exhausts the camp's horror, and that the dignity offended in the camp is not that of life but rather of death. In an interview given to Günther Gaus in 1964, Hannah Arendt thus described her reaction upon learning the truth about the camps, in all its details:

> Before that we said: Well, one has enemies. That is entirely natural. Why shouldn't a people have enemies? But this was different. It was

really as if an abyss had opened. *This ought not to have happened.* And I don't just mean the number of victims. I mean the method, the fabrication of corpses and so on — I don't need to go into that. This should not have happened. Something happened there to which we cannot reconcile ourselves. None of us ever can (Arendt 1993: 13–14).

Every sentence here is charged with a meaning so awful as to compel whoever speaks to have recourse to phrases that stand halfway between euphemism and the unprecedented. First of all, the curious expression repeated in two versions, "this should not have happened," appears at first glance to have at least a resentful tone, which is surprising given its origin on the lips of the author of the most courageous and demystifying book on the problem of evil in our time. The impression grows as one reads the final words: "Something happened there to which we cannot reconcile ourselves. None of us ever can." (Resentment, Nietzsche said, is born from the will's impossibility to accept that something happened, from its incapacity to reconcile itself to time and to time's "so it was.")

Arendt identifies what should not have happened and nevertheless happened immediately afterward. It is something so appalling that, having named it, Arendt makes a gesture bordering on reluctance or shame ("I don't need to go into that"): "the fabrication of corpses and so on." Hilberg informs us that the definition of extermination as a kind of fabrication by "conveyor belt" (*am laufenden Band*) was used for the first time by a physician of the SS, F. Entress. Since then, it has been repeated countless times, often out of context.

In each case, the expression "fabrication of corpses" implies that it is no longer possible truly to speak of death, that what took place in the camps was not death, but rather something infinitely more appalling. In Auschwitz, people did not die; rather, corpses were produced. Corpses without death, non-humans whose decease is debased into a matter of serial production. And, according to a possible and widespread interpretation, precisely this degradation of death constitutes the specific offense of Auschwitz, the proper name of its horror.

2.19   Yet it is not at all obvious that the degradation of death constitutes the ethical problem of Auschwitz. Whenever Auschwitz is approached from this perspective, certain contradictions arise inevitably. This is already the case with those authors who, many years before Auschwitz, denounced the degradation of death in our time. The first of these authors, of course, is Rilke, who may even constitute the unexpected, more or less direct, source of Entress's expression concerning the chain production of death in the camps. "Now there are 559 beds to die in. Like a factory [*fabrikmässig*], of course. With production so enormous, each individual death is not made very carefully; but that isn't important. It's the quantity that counts" (Rilke 1983: 8–9). And in the same years, Péguy, in a passage that Adorno evoked concerning Auschwitz, spoke of the loss of the dignity of death in the modern world: "the modern world has succeeded in swallowing what is perhaps the hardest thing in the world to swallow, since it is something that in itself, almost in its texture, has a kind of special dignity, something like a particular incapacity to be swallowed: death."

Rilke opposes "serial" death to the "proper death" of good old times, the death that everyone carried within him just "as a fruit has its core" (*ibid.*: 10), the death that "one had" and that "gave to each person special dignity and silent pride." The entire *Book of Poverty and Death*, written in the shock of Rilke's stay in Paris, is dedicated to the degradation of death in the big city, where the impossibility of living becomes the impossibility of bringing to fruition one's own death, the "great death each of us has within us" (Rilke 1995: 90). It is remarkable, though, that if one excludes the obsessive recourse to imagery of childbirth and abortion ("we give birth to our own stillborn death" [*ibid.*: 91]) and bitter and ripe fruit ("this death hangs green, devoid of sweetness, / like a fruit inside them / that never ripens" [*ibid.*: 90]), proper death distinguishes itself from the other kind of death only by the most abstract and formal predicates: proper/improper and internal/external. Faced with the expropriation of death accomplished by modernity, the poet reacts according to Freud's scheme of mourning; he interiorizes the lost object. Or, as in the analogous case of melancholy, by forcing to appear as expropriated an object — death — concerning which it makes no sense to speak either of propriety or impropriety. Nowhere does Rilke say what renders Chamberlain Brigge's death a "princely" and proper death, with the one exception that the Old Brigge dies precisely in *his* house, surrounded by *his* servants and *his* dogs. Rilke's attempt to give back "a special dignity" to death leaves an impression of such indecency that in the end, the peasant's dream to kill his suffering lord "with a dung fork" seems to betray the poet's own repressed desire.

2.20   Before Hannah Arendt, Martin Heidegger, Arendt's teacher in Freiburg in the mid-twenties, had already used the expression "fabrication of corpses" to define the extermination camps. And, curiously enough, for Heidegger the "fabrication of corpses" implied, just as for Levi, that it is not possible to speak of death in the case of extermination victims, that they did not truly die, but were rather only pieces produced in a process of an assembly line production. "They die in masses, hundreds of thousands at a time," reads the text of Heidegger's lecture on technology given in Bremen under the title "The Danger" (*Die Gefahr*).

73

Do they die? They decease. They are eliminated. They become pieces of the warehouse of the fabrication of corpses. They are imperceptibly liquidated in extermination camps.... But to die (*Sterben*) means: to bear death in one's own Being. To be able to die means: to be capable of this decisive bearing. And we are capable of it only if our Being is capable of the Being of death.... Everywhere we face the immense misery of innumerable, atrocious deaths that have not died [*ungestorbener Tode*], and yet the essence of death is closed off to man (Heidegger 1994: 56).

Not without reason, a few years later, the objection was raised that for an author implicated even marginally in Nazism a cursory allusion to the extermination camps after years of silence was, at the very least, out of place. What is certain, however, is that the victims saw the dignity of death to be so negated for them that they were condemned to perish — according to an image recalling Rilke's reference to "aborted deaths" — in a death that is not dead. But what, in the camp, could a *dead* death have been, a death borne in its very Being? And is there truly any sense at Auschwitz in distinguishing a proper death from an improper death?

The fact is that, in *Being and Time*, death is assigned a particular function. Death is the site of a decisive experience that, under the name "Being-towards-death," expresses perhaps the ultimate intention of Heidegger's ethics. For in the "decision" that takes place here, everyday impropriety — made up of chatter, ambiguities, and diversions and in which man finds himself always already thrown — is transformed into propriety; and anonymous death, which always concerns others and is never truly present, becomes the most proper and insuperable possibility. Not that this possibility has a particular content, offering man something to be or to realize. On the contrary, death, considered as possibility, is absolutely empty; it has no particular prestige. It is the simple *possibility of the impossibility of all comportment and all existence.* Precisely for this reason, however, the decision that radically experiences this impossibility and this emptiness in Being-towards-death frees itself from all indecision, fully appropriating its own impropriety for the first time. The experience of the measureless impossibility of existing is therefore the way in which man, liberating himself of his fallenness in the world of the "They" (*das Man*), renders his own factical existence possible.

Auschwitz's position in the Bremen lecture is therefore all the more significant. From this perspective, the camp is the place in which it is impossible to experience death as the most proper and insuperable possibility, as the possibility of the impossible. It is the place, that is, in which there can be no appropriation of the improper and in which the factual dominion of the inauthentic knows neither reversal nor exception. This is why, in the camps (as in the epoch of the unconditional triumph of technology, according to the philosopher), the Being of death is inaccessible and men do not die, but are instead produced as corpses.

Yet one may still wonder if Rilke's model, which rigidly separates proper from improper death, did not produce a contradiction in the philosopher's thinking. In Heidegger's ethics, authenticity and propriety do not hover above inauthentic everydayness, as an ideal realm placed above reality; instead, they are "an emended apprehension of the improper" in which what is made free are simply the factual possibilities of existence. According to Hölderlin's principle often invoked by Heidegger, "where there is danger, there grows the saving power," precisely in the extreme situation of the camp appropriation and freedom ought to be possible.

The reason for which Auschwitz is excluded from the experience of death must be a different one, a reason that calls into question the very possibility of authentic decision and thus threatens the very ground of Heidegger's ethics. In the camp, every distinction between proper and improper, between possible and impossible, radically disappears. For here the principle according to which the sole content of the proper is the improper is exactly verified by its inversion, which has it that the sole content of the improper is the proper. And just as in Being-towards-death, the human being authentically appropriates the inauthentic, so in the camp, the prisoners exist *everyday anonymously* toward death. The appropriation of the improper is no longer possible because the improper has completely assumed the function of the proper; human beings live factually at every instant toward their death. This means that in Auschwitz it is no longer possible to distinguish between death and mere decease, between dying and "being liquidated." "The free person," Améry writes thinking of Heidegger, "can assume a certain spiritual posture toward death, because for him death is not totally absorbed into the torment of dying" (Améry 1980: 18). In the camp this is impossible. And this is so not because, as Améry seems to suggest, the thought of ways of dying (by phenol injection, gas, or beating) renders superfluous the thought of death as such. Rather, it is because where the thought of death has been materially realized, where death is "trivial, bureaucratic, and an everyday affair" (Levi 1989: 148), both death and dying, both dying and its ways, both death and the fabrication of corpses, become indistinguishable.

2.21   Grete Salus, an Auschwitz survivor whose words always sound true, once wrote that "man should never have to bear everything that he can bear, nor should he ever have to see how this suffering to the most extreme power no longer has anything human about it" (Langbein 1988: 96). It is worth reflecting on this singular formulation, which perfectly expresses the specific modal status of the camp, its particular reality, which, according to survivors' testimony, renders it absolutely true and at the same time unimaginable. If in Being-towards-death, it was a matter of creating the possible through the experience of the impossible (the experience of death), here the impossible (mass death) is produced through the full experience of the possible, through the exhaustion of its infinity. This is why the camp is the absolute verification of Nazi politics, which, in the words of Goebbels, was precisely the "art of making possible what seems impossible" (*Politik ist die Kunst, das unmöglich Scheinende möglich zu machen*). And this is why in the camp, the most proper gesture of Heidegger's ethics — the appropriation of the improper, the making possible of existence — remains ineffectual; this is why "the essence of death is closed off to man."

Whoever was in the camp, whether he was drowned or survived, bore everything that he could bear — even what he would not have wanted to or should not have had to bear. This "suffering to the most extreme power," this exhaustion of the possible, nevertheless has nothing "human" about it. Human power borders on the inhuman; the human also endures the non-human. Hence the survivor's unease, the "unceasing discomfort ... that ... was nameless," in which Levi discerns the atavistic anguish of Genesis, "the anguish inscribed in every one of the 'tohu-bohu' of a deserted and empty universe crushed under the spirit of God but from which the spirit of man is absent: not yet born or already extinguished" (Levi 1989: 85). This means that humans bear within themselves the mark of the inhuman, that their spirit contains at its very center the wound of non-spirit, non-human chaos atrociously consigned to its own being capable of everything.

Both the survivor's discomfort and testimony concern not merely what was done or suffered, but what *could* have been done or suffered. It is this *capacity*, this almost infinite potentiality to suffer that is inhuman — not the facts, actions, or omissions. And it is precisely this *capacity* that is denied to the SS. The executioners unanimously continue to repeat that they *could* not do other than as they did, that, in other words, they simply *could* not; they had to, and that is all. In German, to act without being capable of acting is called *Befehlnotstand*, having to obey an order. And they obeyed *kadavergehorsam*, like a corpse, as Eichmann said. Certainly, even the executioners had to bear what they should not have had (and, at times, wanted) to bear; but, according to Karl Valentin's profound witticism, in every case "they did not feel up to being capable of it." This is why they remained "humans"; they did not experience the inhuman. Perhaps never was this radical incapacity to "be able" expressed with such blind clarity as in Himmler's speech of October 4, 1943:

> Most of you know what it means when 100 corpses lie there, or when 500 corpses lie there, or when 1,000 corpses lie there. To have gone through this and — apart from a few exceptions caused by human weakness — to have remained decent, that has made us great. That is a page of glory in our history which has never been written and which will never be written... (Hilberg 1979: 648).

It is not by chance, then, that the SS showed themselves to be almost without exception incapable of bearing witness. While the victims bore witness to their having become inhuman, to having borne everything that they *could* bear, the executioners, while torturing and killing, remained "honest men"; they did not bear what they nevertheless could have borne. And if the extreme figure of this extreme potentiality to suffer is the *Muselmann*, then one understands why the SS could not see the *Muselmann*, let alone bear witness to him. "They were so weak; they let themselves do anything. They were people with whom there was no common ground, no possibility of communication — this is where the contempt came from. I just couldn't imagine how they could give in like that. Recently I read a book on winter rabbits, who every five or six years throw themselves into the sea to die; it made me think of Treblinka" (Sereny 1983: 313).

2.22 The idea that the corpse deserves particular respect, that there is something like a dignity of death, does not truly belong to the field of ethics. Its roots lie instead in the most archaic stratum of law, which is at every point indistinguishable from magic. The honor and care given to the deceased's body was originally intended to keep the soul of the dead person (or, rather, his image or phantasm) from remaining a threatening presence in the world of the living (the *larva* of the Latins and the *eidōlon* or *phantasma* of the Greeks). Funeral rites served precisely to transform this uncomfortable and uncertain being into a friendly and potent ancestor with whom it would then be possible to establish well-defined cultic relations.

The ancient world was, however, familiar with practices that aimed at rendering impossible any reconciliation with the dead. Sometimes it was simply a matter of neutralizing the hostile presence of the phantasm, as in the horrid *mascalismos* ritual, in which the extremities of the corpse of a killed person (hands, nose, ears, etc.) were cut off and strung along a little cord, which was then passed under the armpit so that the dead person could not take revenge for the offenses he suffered. The deprivation of burial (which is at the origin of the tragic conflict between Antigone and Creon) was also a form of magic revenge exerted on the corpse of the dead person, who was thus eternally condemned to remain a *larva*, incapable of finding peace. This is why in archaic Greek and Roman law, the obligation to hold a funeral was so strict that in the absence of a corpse, it was stipulated that a *colossus* — a kind of ritual double of the deceased (usually a wooden or wax effigy) — be burned in its place.

79

In firm opposition to these magical practices stand both the philosopher's statement that "the corpse is to be thrown away like dung" (Heraclitus, fr. 96) and the evangelical precept that enjoins the dead to bury the dead (of which there is an echo, in the Church, in the prohibition of certain Franciscan spiritual currents regarding the officiation of funeral rites). It is even possible to say that from the beginning, the link and alternating contrast of this double heredity — a magico-juridical one and a philosophico-messianic one — determine the ambiguity of our culture's relation to the question of the dignity of death.

Perhaps nowhere does this ambiguity emerge as forcefully as in the episode in *The Brothers Karamazov* in which the corpse of Starets Zosima gives off an intolerable stench. For the monks who crowd around the cell of the holy Starets are soon divided among themselves. Faced with the dead body's obvious lack of dignity — which, instead of emitting a saintly odor, begins to decompose indecently — the majority calls into question the saintliness of Zosima's life; only a few know that the fate of the corpse does not authorize any consequences on the plane of ethics. The smell of putrefaction that blows over the heads of the incredulous monks in some way evokes the nauseating odor that the crematorial ovens — the "ways of heaven" — dispersed over the camps. Here too, for many, this stench is the sign of Auschwitz's supreme offense against the dignity of mortals.

2.23   The ambiguity of our culture's relation to death reaches its paroxysm after Auschwitz. This is particularly evident in Adorno, who wanted to make Auschwitz into a kind of historical watershed, stating not only that "after Auschwitz one cannot write poetry" but even that "all post-Auschwitz culture, including its urgent critique, is garbage" (Adorno 1973: 367). On the one hand, Adorno seems to share Arendt's and Heidegger's considerations (for which otherwise he has no sympathy whatsoever) regarding the "fabrication of corpses"; thus he speaks of a "mass, low cost production of death." But on the other hand, he scornfully denounces Rilke's (and Heidegger's) claims for a proper death. "Rilke's prayer for 'one's own death,'" we read in *Minima Moralia*, "is a piteous way to conceal the fact that nowadays people merely snuff out" (Adorno 1974: 233).

This oscillation betrays reason's incapacity to identify the specific crime of Auschwitz with certainty. Auschwitz stands accused on two apparently contradictory grounds: on the one hand, of having realized the unconditional triumph of death against life; on the other, of having degraded and debased death. Neither of these charges — perhaps like every charge, which is always a genuinely legal gesture — succeed in exhausting Auschwitz's offense, in defining its case in point. It is as if there were in Auschwitz something like a Gorgon's head, which one cannot — and does not want to — see at any cost, something so unprecedented that one tries to make it comprehensible by bringing it back to categories that are both extreme and absolutely familiar: life and death, dignity and indignity. Among these categories, the true cipher of Auschwitz — the *Muselmann*, the "core of the camp," he whom "no one wants to see," and who is inscribed in every testimony as a lacuna — wavers without finding a definite position. He is truly the *larva* that our memory cannot succeed in burying, the unforgettable with whom we must reckon. In one case, he appears as the non-living, as the being whose life is not truly life; in the other, as he whose death cannot be called death, but only the production of a corpse — as the inscription of life in a dead area and, in death, of a living area. In both cases, what is called into question is the very humanity of man, since man observes the fragmentation of his privileged tie to what constitutes him as human, that is, the sacredness of death and life. The *Muselmann* is the non-human who obstinately appears as human; he is the human that cannot be told apart from the inhuman.

If this is true, then what does the survivor mean when he speaks of the *Muselmann* as the "complete witness," the only one for whom testimony would have a general meaning? How can the non-human testify to the human, and how can the true witness be the one who by definition cannot bear witness? The Italian title of *Survival in Auschwitz*, "If This Is a Man," also has this meaning; the name "man" applies first of all to a non-man, and the complete witness is he whose humanity has been wholly destroyed. *The human being*, Levi's title implies, *is the one who can survive the human being*. If we give the name "Levi's paradox" to the statement that "the *Muselmann* is the complete witness," then understanding Auschwitz — if such a thing is possible — will coincide with understanding the sense and nonsense of this paradox.

2.24   Michel Foucault offers an explanation of the degradation of death in our time, an explanation in political terms that ties it to the transformation of power in the modern age. In its traditional form, which is that of territorial sovereignty, power defines itself essentially as the right over life and death. Such a right, however, is by definition asymmetrical in the sense that it exerts itself above all from the side of death; it concerns life only indirectly, as the abstention of the right to kill. This is why Foucault characterizes sovereignty through the formula *to make die and to let live*. When, starting with the seventeenth century and the birth of the science of police, care for the life and health of subjects begins to occupy an increasing place in the mechanisms and calculations of states, sovereign power is progressively transformed into what Foucault calls "biopower." The ancient right to kill and to let live gives way to an inverse model, which defines modern biopolitics, and which can be expressed by the formula *to make live and to let die.* "While in the right of sovereignty death was the point in which the sovereign's absolute power shone most clearly, now death instead becomes the moment in which the individual eludes all power, falling back on himself and somehow bending back on what is most private in him" (Foucault 1997: 221). Hence the progressive disqualification of death, which strips it of its character as a public rite in which not only individuals and families but the whole people participates; hence the transformation of death into something to be hidden, a kind of private shame.

The point at which the two models of power collide is the death of Franco. Here the person who incarnated the ancient sovereign power of life and death for the longest time in our century falls into the hands of the new medical, biopolitical power, which succeeds so well in "making men live" as to make them live even when they are dead. And yet for Foucault the two powers, which in the body of the dictator seem to be momentarily indistinguishable, remain essentially heterogeneous; their distinction gives rise to a series of conceptual oppositions (individual body/population, discipline/mechanisms of regulation, man-body/ man species) that, at the dawn of the modern age, define the passage from one system to the other. Naturally, Foucault is perfectly aware that the two powers and their techniques can, in certain cases, be integrated within each other; but they nevertheless remain conceptually distinct. Yet this very heterogeneity becomes problematic when it is a matter of confronting the analysis of the great totalitarian states of our time, in particular the Nazi state. In Hitler's Germany, an unprecedented absolutization of the biopower to *make live* intersects with an equally absolute generalization of the sovereign power to *make die,* such that biopolitics coincides immediately with thanatopolitics. From the Foucaultian perspective, this coincidence represents a genuine paradox, which, like all paradoxes, demands an explanation. How is it possible that a power whose aim is essentially to make live instead exerts an unconditional power of death?

The answer Foucault gives to this question in his 1976 Collège de France course is that racism is precisely what allows biopower to mark caesuras in the biological continuum of the human species, thus reintroducing a principle of war into the system of "making live." "In the biological continuum of the human species, the opposition and hierarchy of races, the qualification of certain races as good and others, by contrast, as inferior, are all ways to fragment the biological domain whose care power had undertaken; they are ways to distinguish different groups inside a population. In short, to stabilize a caesura of a biological type inside a domain that defines itself precisely as biological" (Foucault 1997: 227).

Let us try to further develop Foucault's analysis. The fundamental caesura that divides the biopolitical domain is that between *people* and *population*, which consists in bringing to light a population in the very bosom of a people, that is, in transforming an essentially political body into an essentially biological body, whose birth and death, health and illness, must then be regulated. With the emergence of biopower, every people is doubled by a population; every *democratic* people is, at the same time, a *demographic* people. In the Nazi Reich, the 1933 legislation on the "protection of the hereditary health of the German people" marks this caesura perfectly. The caesura that immediately follows is the one by which, in the set of all citizens, citizens of "Aryan descent" are distinguished from those of "non-Aryan descent." A further caesura then traverses the set of citizens of "non-Aryan descent," separating Jews (*Volljuden*) from *Mischlinge* (people with only one Jewish grandparent, or with two Jewish grandparents but who neither are of Jewish faith nor have Jewish spouses as of September 15, 1935). Biopolitical caesuras are essentially mobile, and in each case they isolate a further zone in the biological continuum, a zone which corresponds to a process of increasing *Entwürdigung* and degradation. Thus the non-Aryan passes into the Jew, the Jew into the deportee (*umgesiedelt, ausgesiedelt*), the deportee into the prisoner (*Häftling*), until biopolitical caesuras reach their final limit in the camp. This limit is the *Muselmann*. At the point in which the *Häftling* becomes a *Muselmann,* the biopolitics of racism so to speak transcends race, penetrating into a threshold in which it is no longer possible to establish caesuras. Here the wavering link between people and population is definitively broken, and we witness the emergence of something like an absolute biopolitical substance that cannot be assigned to a particular bearer or subject, or be divided by another caesura.

It is then possible to understand the decisive function of the camps in the system of Nazi biopolitics. They are not merely the place of death and extermination; they are also, and above all, the site of the production of the *Muselmann*, the final biopolitical substance to be isolated in the biological continuum. Beyond the *Muselmann* lies only the gas chamber.

In 1937, during a secret meeting, Hitler formulates an extreme biopolitical concept for the first time, one well worth considering. Referring to Central-Western Europe, he claims to need a *volkloser Raum*, a space empty of people. How is one to understand this singular expression? It is not simply a matter of something like a desert, a geographical space empty of inhabitants (the region to which he referred was densely populated by different peoples and nationalities). Hitler's "peopleless space" instead designates a fundamental biopolitical intensity, an intensity that can persist in every space and through which peoples pass into populations and populations pass into *Muselmänner*. *Volkloser Raum*, in other words, names the driving force of the camp understood as a biopolitical machine that, once established in a determinate geographical space, transforms it into an absolute biopolitical space, both *Lebensraum* and *Todesraum*, in which human life transcends every assignable biopolitical identity. Death, at this point, is a simple epiphenomenon.

CHAPTER THREE

Shame, or On the Subject

3.1   At the beginning of *The Reawakening*, Levi describes his encounter with the first Russian advance guard that, at around noon on January 27, 1945, reached the camp of Auschwitz, which the Germans had abandoned. The arrival of the Russian soldiers, which marks the prisoners' definitive liberation from the nightmare, takes place not under the sign of joy but, curiously enough, under that of shame:

> They were four young soldiers on horseback, who advanced along the road that marked the limits of the camp, cautiously holding their sten-guns. When they reached the barbed wire, they stopped to look, exchanging a few timid words, and throwing strangely embarrassed glances at the sprawling bodies, at the battered huts and at us few still alive.... They did not greet us, nor did they smile; they seemed oppressed not only by compassion but by a confused restraint, which sealed their lips and bound their eyes to the funereal scene. It was that shame we knew so well, the shame that drowned us after the selections, and every time we had to watch, or submit to, some outrage: the shame the Germans did not know, that the just man experiences at another man's crime, at the fact that such a crime should exist, that it should have been introduced irrevocably

87

into the world of things that exist, and that his will for good should
have proved too weak or null, and should not have availed in defence
(Levi 1986: 181–82, translation slightly emended).

More than twenty years later, while writing *The Drowned and
the Saved*, Levi once again reflects on this shame. Shame now becomes the dominant sentiment of survivors, and Levi tries to
explain why this is so. It is therefore not surprising that, like all
attempts at explanations, the chapter of the book entitled "Shame"
is ultimately unsatisfying. This is all the more so given that the
chapter immediately follows Levi's extraordinary analysis of the
"gray zone," which, consciously keeping to the inexplicable, reck-
lessly refuses all explanation. Faced with the *Kapos*, collaborators,
"prominent ones" of all kinds, the accursed members of the *Sonderkommando* and even Chaim Rumkowski, the *rex Judaeorum* of
the Lodz ghetto, the survivor ended with a *non-liquet*: "I ask that
we meditate on the story of 'the crematorium ravens' with pity
and rigor, but that judgment of them be suspended" (Levi 1989:
60). But in his chapter on shame Levi seems hastily to lead his
subject back to a sense of guilt: "many (including me) experienced 'shame,' that is, a feeling of guilt." (Levi 1989: 73). Immediately afterward, in seeking to discern the roots of this guilt, the
very author who had only a little earlier fearlessly ventured into
an absolutely unexplored territory of ethics now submits himself
to a test of conscience so puerile that it leaves the reader uneasy.
The wrongs that emerge (having at times shaken his shoulders
impatiently when faced with the requests of younger prisoners,
or the episode of the water that he shared with Alberto but
denied to Daniele) are, of course, excusable. But here the reader's
unease can only be a reflection of the survivor's embarrassment,
his incapacity to master shame.

3.2 The survivor's feeling of guilt is a *locus classicus* of literature on the camps. Bettelheim expressed its paradoxical character:

> the real issue … is that the survivor as a thinking being knows very well that he is not guilty, as I, for one, know about myself, but that this does not change the fact that the humanity of such a person, as a feeling being, requires that he *feel* guilty, and he does. One cannot survive the concentration camp without feeling guilty that one was so incredibly lucky when millions perished, many of them in front of one's eyes…. In the camps one was forced, day after day, for years, to watch the destruction of others, feeling — against one's better judgment — that one should have intervened, feeling guilty for having often felt glad that it was not oneself who perished (Bettelheim 1979: 297–98).

Wiesel formulates the same kind of aporia in the apothegm "I live, therefore I am guilty," adding immediately afterward: "I am here because a friend, an acquaintance, an unknown person died in my place." Ella Lingens offers a similar explanation, as if the survivor could live only in the place of another: "Does not each of us who has returned go around with a guilt feeling, feelings which our executors so rarely feel — 'I live, because others died in my place?'" (Langbein 1972: 539).

Levi also experienced this kind of sentiment. And yet he does not fully accept its consequences; he fights tenaciously against it. The conflict finds expression as late as 1984, in his poem "The Survivor:"

Dopo di allora, ad ora incerta,
Quella pena ritorna,
E se non trova chi lo ascolti,
Gli brucia in petto il cuore.

Rivede i visi dei suoi compagni
Lividi nella prima luce,
Grigi di polvere di cemento,
Indistinti per nebbia,
Tinti di morte nei sonni inquieti:
A notte menano le mascelle
Sotto la mora greve dei sogni
Masticando una rapa che non c'è.
"Indietro, via di qui, gente sommersa,
Andate. Non ho soppiantato nessuno,
No ho usurpato il pane di nessuno,
Nessuno è morto in vece mia. Nessuno.
Ritornate alla vostra nebbia.
Non è mia colpa se vivo e respiro
e mangio e bevo e dormo e vesto panni."

Since then, at an uncertain hour, that punishment comes back. And if it doesn't find someone who will listen to it, it burns his heart in his chest. Once again he sees the faces of the other inmates, blueish in the light of dawn, gray with cement dust, shrouded in mist, painted with death in their restless sleep. At night their jaws grind away, in the absence of dreams, chewing on a stone that isn't there. "Get away from here, drowned people, go away. I didn't ursurp anyone's place. I didn't steal anyone's bread. No one died in my stead. No one. Go back to your mist. It isn't my fault if I live and breathe, eat and drink and sleep and wear clothes" (Levi 1988: 581).

The citation from Dante in the last verse bears witness to the fact that what is at issue in this text is not simply the disavowal of responsibility. The citation comes from the thirty-third canto of the *Inferno* (v. 141), which describes Dante's encounter with

Ugolino in the traitors' pit. It contains a double, implicit reference to the problem of the guilt of the deportees. On the one hand, Dante's "dark well" is the place of traitors, in particular those who have betrayed their own relatives and friends. On the another hand, in a bitter allusion to his own situation as a survivor, the cited verse also refers to someone whom Dante believes to be alive, but who is only apparently living, since his soul has already been swallowed by death.

Two years later, when he writes *The Drowned and the Saved*, Levi once again asks himself the following question: "Are you ashamed because you are alive in place of another? And in particular, of a man more generous, more sensitive, more useful, wiser, worthier of living than you?" But this time too the answer is doubtful:

> You cannot block out such feelings: you examine yourself, you review your memories, hoping to find them all, and that none of them are masked or disguised. No, you find no obvious transgressions, you did not usurp anyone's place, you did not beat anyone (but would you have had the strength to do so?), you did not accept positions (but none were offered to you...), you did not steal anyone's bread; nevertheless you cannot exclude it. It is no more than a supposition, indeed the shadow of a suspicion: that each man is his brother's Cain, that each one of us (but this time I say "us" in a much vaster, indeed, universal sense) has usurped his neighbor's place and lived in his stead (Levi 1989: 81–82).

Yet the same generalization of the accusation (or, rather, the suspicion) somehow blunts its edge; it makes the wound less painful. "No one died in my stead. No one" (Levi 1988: 581). "One is never in the place of another" (Levi 1989: 60).

3.3   The other face of the survivor's shame is the exaltation of simple survival as such. In 1976, Terrence Des Pres, professor at Colgate University, published *The Survivor: An Anatomy of Life in the Death Camps*. The book, which had an immediate and notable success, set out to show that "survival is an experience with a definite structure, neither random nor regressive nor amoral" (Des Pres 1976: v) and, at the same time, to "render visible that structure" (*ibid.*). In the final analysis, Des Pres's anatomical dissection of life in the camps reveals that in the final analysis life is survival and that in the extreme situation of Auschwitz, the very nucleus of "life in itself" comes to light as such, freed from the hindrances and deformations of culture. Des Pres does, at a certain point, invoke the specter of the *Muselmann* as a figure representing the impossibility of survival ("the empirical instance of death-in-life" [*ibid.*: 99]). But he criticizes Bettelheim's testimony for having undervalued the prisoners' anonymous and everyday fight to survive, in the name of an antiquated ethics of the hero, of the one who is ready to renounce his life. For Des Pres, the true ethical paradigm of our time is instead the survivor, who, without searching for ideal justifications "chooses life" and fights simply to survive. The survivor, he writes,

> is the first of civilized men to live beyond the compulsions of culture; beyond a fear of death which can only be assuaged by insisting that life itself is worthless. The survivor is evidence that men and women are strong enough, mature enough, awake enough, to face death without mediation, and therefore to embrace life without reserve (*ibid.*: 245).

The life that the survivor chooses to "embrace without reservations," the "small, additional, added-on life" (*ibid.*: 24), for which he is ready to pay the highest price, reveals itself in the end to be nothing other than biological life as such, the simple, impenetrable "priority of the biological element." With a perfect vicious circle in which to continue is nothing other than to go backward, the "additional life" disclosed by survival is simply an absolute a priori:

> Stripped of everything but life, what can the survivor fall back upon except some biologically determined "talent" long suppressed by cultural deformation, a bank of knowledge embedded in the body's cells. The key to survival behavior may thus lie in the priority of biological being (*ibid.*: 228).

3.4 It is not surprising that Bettelheim reacted to Des Pres's book with indignation. In an article that appeared in *The New Yorker* following the publication of *The Survivor*, Bettelheim reaffirms the decisive importance of the survivor's feeling of guilt:

> It will be startling news to most survivors that they are "strong enough, mature enough, awake enough...to embrace life without reserve," since only a pitifully small number of those who entered the German camps survived. What about the millions who perished? Were they "awake enough...to embrace life without reserve" as they were driven into the gas chambers?...What about the many survivors who were completely broken by their experience, so that years of the best psychiatric care could not help them cope with their memories, which continue to haunt them in their deep and often suicidal depression?...What of the horrible nightmares about the camps which every so often awaken me today, thirty-five years later, despite a most rewarding life, and which every survivor I have asked has also experienced?...Only the ability to feel guilty makes us human, particularly if, objectively seen, one is not guilty (Bettelheim 1979: 296, 313).

Despite their polemical tones, the two adversaries are in fact not as far apart as they seem; they are, more or less consciously, both prisoners of a curious circle. On the one hand, the exaltation of survival constantly requires reference to dignity ("There is a strange circularity about existence in extremity: survivors preserve their dignity in order 'not to begin to die'; they care for the body as a matter of 'moral survival'" [Des Pres 1976: 72]). On the other hand, the assertion of dignity and the feeling of guilt have no other sense than survival and "the life instinct" ("those prisoners who blocked out neither heart nor reason... those prisoners survived" [Bettelheim 1960: 158]; "Our obligation — not to those who are dead, but to ourselves, and to those around us who are still alive — is to strengthen the life drives" [Bettelheim 1979: 102]). And it is certainly not an accident that Bettelheim ends by accusing Des Pres of the same "ethics of heroism" with which Des Pres had earlier criticized Bettelheim: "[Des Pres's book] makes heroes out of these chance survivors. By stressing how the death camps produced such superior beings as the survivors..." (*ibid.*: 95).

It is as if the symmetrical gestures of the two opposite figures of the survivor — the one who cannot feel guilty for his own survival and the one who claims innocence in having survived — betrayed a secret solidarity. They are the two faces of the living being's incapacity truly to separate innocence and guilt — that is, somehow to master its own shame.

3.5   It is uncertain whether the correct explanation for the survivor's shame is that he feels guilty for being alive in the place of another. Bettelheim's thesis that the survivor is innocent and yet as such obliged to feel guilty is itself already suspect. To assume guilt of this kind, which inheres in the survivor's condition as such and not in what he or she as an individual did or failed to do, recalls the common tendency to assume a generic collective guilt whenever an ethical problem cannot be mastered. Arendt observed that the surprising willingness of post-war Germans of all ages to assume collective guilt for Nazism, to believe themselves guilty for what their parents or their people had done, betrayed an equally surprising ill will as to the assessment of individual responsibilities and the punishment of particular crimes. Analogously, at a certain point the German Protestant Church publicly declared itself "complicit before the God of Mercy for the evil that our people did to the Jews." But the Protestant Church was not so ready to draw the inevitable consequence that this responsibility in reality concerned not the God of Mercy but the God of Justice and should have called for the punishment of those preachers guilty of having justified anti-Semitism. The same can be said for the Catholic Church, which, even recently in the declaration of the French episcopate, showed itself willing to recognize its own collective guilt toward the Jews. Yet this very church has never wanted to admit the precise, grave, and documented omissions of Pope Pius XII with respect to the persecution and extermination of Jews (in particular, with respect to the deportation of Roman Jews in 1943).

Levi is perfectly convinced that it makes no sense to speak of collective guilt (or innocence) and that only metaphorically can one claim to feel guilty for what one's own people or parents did. When a German writes him, not without hypocrisy, that "the guilt weighs heavily on my poor betrayed and misguided people," Levi responds that "one must answer personally for sins and errors, otherwise all trace of civilization would vanish from the face of the earth" (Levi 1989: 177–78). And the only time Levi does speak of collective guilt, he means it in the only sense possible for him, that is, as a wrong committed by "almost all the Germans of the time": of not having had the courage to speak, to bear witness to what they could not not have seen.

95

3.6   But another reason leads one to distrust that explanation. More or less consciously and more or less explicitly, it claims to present the survivor's shame as a tragic conflict. Beginning with Hegel, the guilty-innocent person is the figure through which modern culture interprets Greek tragedy and, concomitantly, its own secret contradictions. "In considering all these tragic conflicts," Hegel writes, "we must above all reject the false idea that they have anything to do with guilt or innocence. The tragic heroes are just as much innocent as guilty" (Hegel 1975: 1214). The conflict of which Hegel speaks, however, is not merely a matter of consciousness, in which subjective innocence is simply opposed to objective guilt. What is tragic is, on the contrary, for an apparently innocent subject to assume unconditionally objective guilt. Thus in *Oedipus Rex*

> what is at issue ... is the right of the wide awake consciousness, the justification of what the man has self-consciously willed and knowingly done, as contrasted with what he was fated by the gods to do and actually did unconsciously and without having willed it. Oedipus has killed his father; he has married his mother and begotten children in this incestuous alliance; and yet he has been involved in these most evil crimes without either knowing or willing them. The right of our deeper consciousness today would consist in recognizing that since he had neither intended nor known these crimes himself, they were not to be regarded as his own deeds. But the Greek, with his plasticity of consciousness, takes responsibility for what he has done as an individual and does not cut his purely subjective self-consciousness apart from what is objectively the case.... But they do not claim to be innocent of these [acts] at all. On the contrary, what they did, and actually had to do, is their glory. No worse insult could be given to such a hero than to say that he had acted innocently (*ibid.*: 1214, 1215).

Nothing is further from Auschwitz than this model. For the deportee sees such a widening of the abyss between subjective innocence and objective guilt, between what he did do and what he could feel responsible for, that he cannot assume responsibility for any of his actions. With an inversion that borders on parody, he feels innocent precisely for that which the tragic hero feels guilty, and guilty exactly where the tragic hero feels innocent. This is the sense of the specific *Befehlnotstand*, the "state of compulsion that follows an order" of which Levi speaks in discussing the *Sonderkommando* members, which makes any tragic conflict at Auschwitz impossible. The objective element, which for the Greek hero was in every case the decisive question, here becomes what renders decision impossible. And since he cannot master his own actions, the victim seeks shelter, like Bettelheim, behind the prestigious mask of innocent guilt.

The ease with which the executioners invoke the tragic model, not always in bad faith, provokes distrust in their capacity truly to give reasons for Auschwitz. It has been observed many times that the Nazi functionaries' recourse to *Befehlnotstand* was in itself impudent (among others, cf. Levi 1989: 59). And yet it is certain that at least from a certain point onward, they invoked it not so much to escape condemnation (the objection was already dismissed during the first Nuremberg trial, given that the German military code itself contained an article authorizing disobedience in extreme cases) as, rather, to make their situation appear in terms of a tragic conflict, which was to their eyes clearly more acceptable. "My client feels guilty before God, not the law," Eichmann's lawyer repeated in Jerusalem.

An exemplary case is that of Fritz Stangl, the commander of the Treblinka extermination camp, whose personality Gitta Sereny patiently sought to reconstruct through a series of interviews held in the Düsseldorf prison, published under the significant title *Into that Darkness*. Until the end, Stangl stubbornly maintained his innocence for the crimes attributed to him, without questioning them in the slightest as to their factual accuracy. But during the last interview on June 27, 1971, a few hours before he died from a heart attack, Sereny remarks that Stangl's last resistances have crumbled and that something like a glimmer of ethical conscience appears "in that darkness":

> "My conscience is clear about what I did, myself," he said, in the same stiffly spoken words he had used countless times at his trial, and in the past weeks, when we had always come back to this subject, over and over again. But this time I said nothing. He paused and waited, but the room remained silent. "I have never intentionally hurt anyone, myself," he said, with a different, less incisive emphasis, and waited again — for a long time. For the first time, in all these many days, I had given him no help. There was no more time. He gripped the table with both hands as if he was holding on to it. "But I was there," he said then, in a curiously dry and tired tone of resignation. These few sentences had taken almost half an hour to pronounce. "So yes," he said finally, very quietly, "in reality I share the guilt.... Because my guilt... my guilt... only now in these talks... now that I have talked about it for the first time...." He stopped.
>
> He had pronounced the words "my guilt": but more than the words, the finality of it was in the sagging of his body, and on his face.
>
> After more than a minute he started again, a half-hearted attempt, in a dull voice. "My guilt," he said, "is that I am still here. That is my guilt" (Sereny 1983: 364).

It is remarkable to hear this allusive evocation of a tragic conflict of a new kind, one so inextricable and enigmatic as to be justly dissolved only by death, from a man who had directed the killing of thousands of human beings in gas chambers. It does not signify the emergence of an instance of truth, in which Stangl "became the man whom he should have been" (*ibid.*: 366), as Sereny, solely concerned with her dialectic of confession and guilt, seems to think. Instead, it marks the definitive ruin of his capacity to bear witness, the despairing collapse of "that darkness" on itself. The Greek hero has left us forever; he can no longer bear witness for us in any way. After Auschwitz, it is not possible to use a tragic paradigm in ethics.

3.7   The ethics of the twentieth century opens with Nietzsche's overcoming of resentment. Against the impotence of the will with respect to the past, against the spirit of revenge for what has irrevocably taken place and can no longer be willed, Zarathustra teaches men to will backward, to desire that everything repeat itself. The critique of Judeo-Christian morality is completed in our century in the name of a capacity fully to assume the past, liberating oneself once and for all of guilt and bad conscience. The eternal return is above all victory over resentment, the possibility of willing what has taken place, transforming every "it was" into a "thus I wanted it to be" — *amor fati.*

Auschwitz also marks a decisive rupture in this respect. Let us imagine repeating the experiment that Nietzsche, under the heading "The Heaviest Weight," proposes in *The Gay Science.* "One day or one night," a demon glides beside a survivor and asks: "Do you want Auschwitz to return again and again, innumerable times, do you want every instant, every single detail of the camp to repeat itself for eternity, returning eternally in the same precise sequence in which they took place? Do you want this to happen again, again and again for eternity?" This simple reformulation of the experiment suffices to refute it beyond all doubt, excluding the possibility of its even being proposed.

Yet this failure of twentieth-century ethics does not depend on the fact that what happened at Auschwitz is too atrocious for anyone ever to wish for its repetition and to love it as destiny. In Nietzsche's experiment, the horror of what happened appears at the start, indeed, so much so that the first effect of listening to it is, precisely, to "gnash one's teeth and curse the demon who has spoken in such way." Nor can one say that the failure of Zarathustra's lesson implies the pure and simple restoration of the morality of resentment — even if, for the victims, the temptation is great. Jean Améry was thus led to formulate a genuine anti-Nietzschean ethics of resentment that simply refuses to accept that "what happened, happened" (Améry 1980: 72). "Resentments as the existential dominant of people like myself," he writes,

> are the result of a long personal and historical development.... My resentments are there in order that the crime become a moral reality for the criminal, in order that he be swept into the truth of his atrocity.... In two decades of contemplating what happened to me, I believe to have recognized that a forgiving and forgetting induced by social pressure is immoral.... Natural consciousness of time actually is rooted in the physiological process of wound-healing and became part of the social conception of reality. But precisely for this reason it is not only extramoral, but also *anti*moral in character. Man has the right and the privilege to declare himself to be in disagreement with every natural occurrence, including the biological healing that time brings about. What happened, happened. This sentence is just as true as it is hostile to mortals and intellect.... The moral person demands annulment of time — in the particular case under question, by nailing the criminal to his deed. Thereby, and through a moral turning-back of the clock, the latter can join his victim as a fellow human being (*ibid.*: 64, 70, 72).

There is nothing of this in Primo Levi. Naturally he rejects the title of "the forgiver" which Améry attributes to him. "I am not inclined to forgive, I never forgave our enemies of that time" (Levi 1989: 137). And yet for him, the impossibility of wanting Auschwitz to return for eternity has another, different root, one which implies a new, unprecedented ontological consistency of what has taken place. *One cannot want Auschwitz to return for eternity, since in truth it has never ceased to take place; it is always already repeating itself.* This ferocious, implacable experience appears to Levi in the form of a dream:

It is a dream within other dreams, which varies in its details but not in its content. I am seated at the dinner table with my family, or with friends, or at work, or in the countryside — in a surrounding that is, in other words, peaceful and relaxed, apparently without tension and suffering. And yet I feel anguish, an anguish that is subtle but deep, the definite sensation of some threat. And, in fact, as the dream continues, bit by bit or all of a sudden — each time it's different — everything falls apart around me, the setting, the walls, the people. The anguish becomes more intense and pronounced. Everything is now in chaos. I'm alone at the center of a gray, cloudy emptiness, and at once I *know* what it means, I know that I've always known it: I am once again in the camp, and nothing outside the camp was true. The rest — family, flowering nature, home — was a brief respite, a trick of the senses. Now this inner dream, this dream of peace, is over; and in the outer dream, which continues relentlessly, I hear the sound of a voice I know well: the sound of one word, not a command, but a brief, submissive word. It is the order at dawn in Auschwitz, a foreign word, a word that is feared and expected: "Get up," *Wstawac* (Levi 1988: 245–55, translation emended).

In the version recorded in the poem *At an Uncertain Hour*, the experience has the form not of a dream, but of a prophetic certainty:

Sognavamo nelle notti feroci
sogni densi e violenti
sognati con anima e corpo:
tornare, mangiare; raccontare.
Finché suonava breve e sommesso
il comando dell'alba:
"Wstawac";
e si spezzava in petto il cuore.
Ora abbiamo ritrovato la casa,
il nostro ventre è sazio,
abbiamo finito di raccontare.
È tempo. Presto udremo ancora
il comando straniero:
"Wstawac."

In savage nights, we dreamt teeming, violent dreams with our body and soul: to go back, to eat — to tell. Until we heard the brief and submissive order of dawn: *Wstawac*. And our hearts were broken in our chests.

Now we have found our homes again; our bellies are full; we have finished telling our tales. It's time. Soon we will once again hear the foreign order: *Wstawac* (Levi 1988: 530).

In this text, the ethical problem has radically changed shape. It is no longer a question of conquering the spirit of revenge in order to assume the past, willing its return for eternity; nor is it a matter of holding fast to the unacceptable through resentment. What lies before us now is a being beyond acceptance and refusal, beyond the eternal past and the eternal present — an event that returns eternally but that, precisely for this reason, is absolutely, eternally unassumable. Beyond good and evil lies not the innocence of becoming but, rather, a shame that is not only without guilt but even without time.

3.8   Antelme clearly bears witness to the fact that shame is not a feeling of guilt or shame for having survived another but, rather, has a different, darker and more difficult cause. He relates that when the war was nearing its end, during the mad march to transfer prisoners from Buchenwald to Dachau, as the Allies were quickly approaching, the SS shot to death all those who would have slowed down the march because of their physical condition. At times the decimation would take place by chance, in the absence of any visible criterion. One day it was a young Italian's turn:

> The SS continues. "*Du komme hier!*" Another Italian steps out of the column, a student from Bologna. I know him. His face has turned pink. I look at him closely. I still have that pink before my eyes. He stands there at the side of the road. He doesn't know what to do with his hands. . . . He turned pink after the SS man said to him, "*Du komme hier!*" He must have glanced about him before he flushed; but yes, it was he who had been picked, and when he doubted it no longer, he turned pink. The SS who was looking for a man, any man, to kill, had found him. And having found him, he looked no further. He didn't ask himself: Why him, instead of someone else? And the Italian, having understood it was really him, accepted this chance selection. He didn't wonder: Why me, instead of someone else? (Antelme 1992: 231–32).

It is hard to forget the flush of the student of Bologna, who died during the march alone at the last minute, on the side of the road with his murderer. And certainly the intimacy that one experiences before one's own unknown murderer is the most extreme intimacy, an intimacy that can as such provoke shame. But whatever the cause of that flush, it is certain that he is not ashamed for having survived. Rather, it is as if he were ashamed for having to die, for having been haphazardly chosen — he and no one else — to be killed. In the camps, this is the only sense that the expression "to die in place of another" can have: everyone dies and lives in place of another, without reason or meaning; the camp is the place in which no one can truly die or survive in his own place. Auschwitz also means this much: that man, dying, cannot find any other sense in his death than this flush, this shame.

In any case, the student is not ashamed for having survived. On the contrary, what survives him is shame. Here, too, Kafka was a good prophet. At the end of *The Trial*, at the moment in which Josef K. is about to die "like a dog," and in which the knife of the executioner turns twice in his heart, something like shame arises in him; "it was as if his shame were to survive him." What is Josef K. ashamed of? Why does the student from Bologna blush? It is as if the flush on his cheeks momentarily betrayed a limit that was reached, as if something like a new ethical material were touched upon in the living being. Naturally it is not a matter of a fact to which he could bear witness otherwise, which he might also have expressed through words. But in any case that flush is like a mute apostrophe flying through time to reach us, to bear witness to him.

3.9   In 1935, Levinas provided an exemplary analysis of shame. According to Levinas, shame does not derive, as the moral philosophers maintain, from the consciousness of an imperfection or a lack in our being from which we take distance. On the contrary, shame is grounded in our being's incapacity to move away and break from itself. If we experience shame in nudity, it is because we cannot hide what we would like to remove from the field of vision; it is because the unrestrainable impulse to flee from oneself is confronted by an equally certain impossibility of evasion. Just as we experience our revolting and yet unsuppressible presence to ourselves in bodily need and nausea, which Levinas classifies alongside shame in a single diagnosis, so in shame we are consigned to something from which we cannot in any way distance ourselves.

> What appears in shame is therefore precisely the fact of being chained to oneself, the radical impossibility of fleeing oneself to hide oneself from oneself, the intolerable presence of the self to itself. Nudity is shameful when it is the obviousness of our Being, of its final intimacy. And the nudity of our body is not the nudity of a material thing that is antithetical to the spirit but the nudity of our entire Being, in all its plenitude and solidity, in its most brutal expression, of which one cannot not be aware. The whistle that Charlie Chaplin swallows in *City Lights* makes appear the scandal of the brutal presence of his Being; it is like a recording device that allows one to lay bare the discrete signs of a presence that the legendary Charlot cloak barely hides.... What is shameful is our intimacy, that is, our presence to ourselves. It reveals not our nothingness but the totality of our existence.... What shame discovers is the Being that *discovers* itself (Levinas 1982: 87).

Let us seek to deepen Levinas's analysis. To be ashamed means to be consigned to something that cannot be assumed. But what cannot be assumed is not something external. Rather, it originates in our own intimacy; it is what is most intimate in us (for example, our own physiological life). Here the "I" is thus overcome by its own passivity, its ownmost sensibility; yet this expropriation and desubjectification is also an extreme and irreducible presence of the "I" to itself. It is as if our consciousness collapsed and, seeking to flee in all directions, were simultaneously summoned by an irrefutable order to be present at its own defacement, at the expropriation of what is most its own. In shame, the subject thus has no other content than its own desubjectification; it becomes witness to its own disorder, its own oblivion as a subject. This double movement, which is both subjectification and desubjectification, is shame.

3.10   In his 1942–43 lecture course on *Parmenides*, Heidegger was also concerned with shame or, more precisely, with the corresponding Greek term *aidos*, which he defined as "a fundamental word of authentic Greekness" (Heidegger 1992: 74–75, translation modified). According to Heidegger, shame is something more than "a feeling that man has" (*ibid.,* translation modified); instead, it is an emotive tonality that traverses and determines his whole Being. Shame is thus a kind of ontological sentiment that has its characteristic place in the encounter between man and Being. It is so little a matter of a psychological phenomenon that Heidegger can write that "Being itself carries with itself shame, the shame of Being" (*ibid.*, translation modified).

To emphasize this ontological character of shame — the fact that, in shame, we find ourselves exposed in the face of Being, which is itself ashamed — Heidegger suggests that we consider disgust (*Abscheu*). Curiously enough, he does not proceed to develop this point, as if it were immediately obvious, which is not at all the case. Fortunately, Benjamin offers an analysis of disgust that is both brief and pertinent in an aphorism of *One-Way Street*. For Benjamin, the predominant feeling in disgust is the fear of being recognized by what repulses us. "The horror that stirs deep in man is an obscure awareness that in him something lives so akin to the animal that it might be recognized" (Benjamin 1979: 50). Whoever experiences disgust has in some way recognized himself in the object of his loathing and fears being recognized in turn. The man who experiences disgust recognizes himself in an alterity that cannot be assumed — that is, he subjectifies himself in an absolute desubjectification.

We find a reciprocity of this kind again in the analysis that Kerényi, more or less in the same years, dedicates to *aidos* in his book, *Ancient Religion*. "The phenomenon of *aidos*, a fundamental situation of the Greeks' religious experience, unites respectively active vision and passive vision, the man who sees and is seen, the seen world and the seeing world — where to see is also to penetrate....The Greek is not only 'born to see,' 'called to see;' the form of his existence is to be seen" (Kerényi 1940: 88). In this reciprocity of active and passive vision, *aidos* resembles the experience of being present at one's own being seen, being taken as a witness by what one sees. Like Hector confronted by his mother's bare chest ("Hector, my son, feel *aidos* for this!"), whoever experiences shame is overcome by his own being subject to vision; he must respond to what deprives him of speech.

We can therefore propose a first, provisional definition of shame. It is nothing less than the fundamental sentiment of being *a subject*, in the two apparently opposed senses of this phrase: to be subjected and to be sovereign. Shame is what is produced in the absolute concomitance of subjectification and desubjectification, self-loss and self-possession, servitude and sovereignty.

3.11   A specific domain exists in which this paradoxical character of shame is consciously taken as an object to be transformed into pleasure — in which shame is, as it were, carried beyond itself. This is the domain of sadomasochism. Here the passive subject, the masochist, is so overtaken by his own passivity, which infinitely transcends him, that he abdicates his condition as a subject by fully subjecting himself to another subject, the sadist. Hence the ceremonial panoply of lace, contracts, metals, girdles, sutures, and constrictions of all kinds through which the masochistic subject vainly tries to contain and ironically fix the very passivity which he cannot assume and which everywhere exceeds him. Only because the masochist's own suffering is first of all that of not being able to assume his own receptivity can his pain be immediately transformed into delight. But what constitutes the subtlety of the masochistic strategy and its almost sarcastic profundity is that the masochist is able to enjoy what exceeds him only on the condition of finding outside himself a point in which he can assume his own passivity and his own unassumable pleasure. This external point is the sadistic subject, the master.

Sadomasochism thus appears as a bipolar system in which an infinite receptivity — the masochist — encounters an equally infinite impassivity — the sadist — and in which subjectification and desubjectification incessantly circulate between two poles without properly belonging to either. This indetermination, however, invests subjects not merely with power, but also with knowledge. The master-slave dialectic here is the result not of a battle for life and death, but rather of an infinite "discipline," a meticulous and interminable process of instruction and apprenticeship in which the two subjects end by exchanging their roles. Just as the masochistic subject cannot assume his pleasure except in the master, so the sadistic subject cannot recognize himself as such — cannot assume his impassive knowledge — if not by transmitting pleasure to the slave through infinite instruction and punishment. But since the masochistic subject enjoys his cruel training by definition, what was to be the instrument of the transmission of knowledge — punishment — is instead the instrument of pleasure; and discipline and apprenticeship, teacher and pupil, master and

slave become wholly indistinguishable. This indistinction of discipline and enjoyment, in which the two subjects momentarily coincide, is precisely shame. And it is this shame that the indignant
master continually recalls to his humorous pupil: "Tell me, aren't
you ashamed?" That is: "Don't you realize that you are the subject
of your own desubjectification?"

3.12   A perfect equivalent of shame can be found precisely in the
originary structure of subjectivity that modern philosophy calls
auto-affection and that, from Kant onward, is generally identified
as time. According to Kant, what defines time as the form of
inner sense, that is, "the intuition of ourselves and of our inner
state" (Kant 1929: 77), is that in it "the understanding...per-
forms this act upon the *passive* subject, whose *faculty* it is, and we
are therefore justified in saying that inner sense is affected thereby" (*ibid.*: 166) and that therefore in time "we intuit ourselves
only as we are inwardly affected *by ourselves*" (*ibid.*: 168). For
Kant, a clear proof of this self-modification implicit in our intuition of ourselves is that we cannot conceive of time without
drawing a straight line in the imagination, a line which is the
immediate trace of the auto-affective gesture. In this sense, time
is auto-affection; but precisely for this reason Kant can speak here
of a genuine "paradox," which consists in the fact that we "must
behave toward ourselves as passive" (*wir uns gegen uns selbst als
leidend verhalten mussten*) (*ibid.*).

How are we to understand this paradox? What does it mean to
be passive with respect to oneself? Passivity does not simply mean
receptivity, the mere fact of being affected by an external active
principle. Since everything takes place here inside the subject,
activity and passivity must coincide. The passive subject must be
active with respect to its own passivity; it must "behave" (*verhalten*) "against" itself (*gegen uns selbst*) as passive. If we define as

merely receptive the photographic print struck by light, or the soft wax on which the image of the seal is imprinted, we will then give the name "passive" only to what actively feels its own being passive, to *what is affected by its own receptivity*. As auto-affection, passivity is thus a receptivity to the second degree, a receptivity that experiences itself, that is moved by its own passivity.

Commenting on these pages of Kant, Heidegger defines time as "pure auto-affection" that has the singular form of a "moving from itself toward..." that is at the same time a "looking back." Only in this complicated gesture, in this looking to oneself in distancing oneself from oneself, can something like an identical self be constituted:

> Time is not an active affection that strikes an already existing subject. As pure auto-affection, it forms the very essence of what can be defined as seeing oneself in general.... But the self itself that, as such, can be seen by something is, in essence, the finite subject. Insofar as it is pure auto-affection, time forms the essential structure of subjectivity. Only on the basis of this selfhood can finite Being be what it must be: delivered over to receiving (Heidegger 1990: 132–31, translation modified).

Here what is revealed is the analogy with shame, defined as being consigned to a passivity that cannot be assumed. Shame, indeed, then appears as the most proper emotive tonality of subjectivity. For there is certainly nothing shameful in a human being who suffers on account of sexual violence; but if he takes pleasure in his suffering violence, if he is moved by his passivity — if, that is, auto-affection is produced — only then can one speak of shame. This is why the Greeks clearly separated, in the homosexual relation, the active subject (the *erastēs*) and the passive subject (*eromenos*) and, for the sake of the ethicity of the relation, demanded that the *eromenos* not experience pleasure. Passivity, as the form of subjectivity, is thus constitutively fractured into a purely receptive pole (the *Muselmann*) and an actively passive pole (the witness), but in such a way that this fracture never leaves itself, fully separating the two poles. On the contrary, it always has the form of an *intimacy*, of being consigned to a passivity, to a making oneself passive in which the two terms are both distinct and inseparable.

In his *Compendium grammaticus linguae hebraeae*, Spinoza illustrates the concept of immanent cause — that is, an action in which agent and patient are one and the same person — with the Hebrew verbal categories of the active reflexive and the infinitive noun. "Since it often happens," he writes, referring to the infinitive noun, "that the agent and the patient are one and the same person, the Jews found it necessary to form a new and seventh kind of infinitive with which to express an action referred both to the agent and the patient, an action that thus has the form both of an activity and a passivity.... It was therefore necessary to invent another kind of infinitive, expressing an action referred to the agent as immanent cause ... which, as we have seen, means 'to visit oneself,' or 'to constitute oneself as visiting' or, finally, 'to show oneself as visiting' (*constituere se visitantem, vel denique praebere se visitantem*)" (Spinoza 1925: 361). Explaining the meaning of these verbal forms, Spinoza is not satisfied with the reflexive form "to visit oneself," and is compelled to form the striking syntagm "to constitute oneself as visiting" or "to show oneself as visiting" (he could also have written "to constitute or show oneself as visited"). Just as in ordinary language, to define someone who takes pleasure in undergoing something (or who is somehow an accomplice to this undergoing) one says that he "gets himself done" something (and not simply that something "is done to him"), so the coincidence of agent and patient in one subject has the form not of an inert identity, but of a complex movement of auto-affection in which the subject constitutes — or shows — itself as passive (or active), such that activity and passivity can never be separated, revealing themselves to be distinct in their impossible coincidence in a *self*. The *self* is what is produced as a remainder in the double movement — active and passive — of auto-affection. This is why subjectivity constitutively has the form of subjectification and desubjectification; this is why it is, at bottom, shame. Flush is the remainder that, in every subjectification, betrays a desubjectification and that, in every desubjectification, bears witness to a subject.

3.13   There is an exceptional document of desubjectification as a shameful and yet inevitable experience. It is the letter Keats sends to John Woodhouse on October 27, 1818. The "wretched confession" of which the letter speaks concerns the poetic subject himself, the incessant self-loss by which he consists solely in alienation and non-existence. The theses that the letter states in the form of paradoxes are well known:

1) *The poetic "I" is not an "I"; it is not identical to itself*: "As to the poetical Character (I mean that sort of which, if I am any thing, I am a Member ...) it is not itself — it has no self — it is every thing and nothing — It has no character" (Keats 1935: 226).

2) *The poet is the most unpoetical of things*, since he is always other than himself; he is always the place of another body: "A Poet is the most unpoetical of any thing in existence; because he has no Identity — he is continually filling in for — and filling some other Body" (*ibid.*: 227).

3) *The statement "I am a poet" is not a statement*, but rather a contradiction in terms, which implies the impossibility of being a poet: "If then he has no self, and if I am a Poet, where is the Wonder that I should say I would write no more?" (*ibid.*).

4) *The poetic experience is the shameful experience of desubjectification*, of a full and unrestrained impossibility of responsibility that involves every act of speech and that situates the would-be poet in a position even lower than that of children: "It is a wretched thing to confess; but it is a very fact that not one word I ever utter can be taken for granted as an opinion growing out of my identical nature — how can it, when I have no nature? When I am in a room with People if I ever am free from speculating on creations of my own brain, then not myself goes home to myself: but the identity of every one in the room begins so to press upon me that I am in a very little time annihilated — not only among Men; it would be the same in a Nursury of children" (*ibid.*).

But the final paradox is that in the letter the confession is immediately followed not only by silence and renunciation, but also by the promise of an absolute and unfailing writing destined to destroy and renew itself day after day. It is almost as if the shame and desubjectification implicit in the act of speech contained a secret beauty that could only bring the poet incessantly to bear witness to his own alienation: "I will assay to reach to as high a summit in Poetry as the nerve bestowed upon me will suffer.... I feel assured I should write ... even if my night's labours should be burnt every morning, and no eye ever shine upon them. But even now I am perhaps not speaking from myself: but from some character in whose soul I now live" (*ibid.*: 227–28).

3.14 In the Western literary tradition, the act of poetic creation and, indeed, perhaps every act of speech implies something like a desubjectification (poets have named this desubjectification the "Muse"). "An 'I' without guarantees!" writes Ingeborg Bachmann in one of her *Frankfurt Lectures*, "what is the 'I,' what could it be? A star whose position and orbit have never been fully identified and whose nucleus is composed of substances still unknown to us. It could be this: myriads of particles forming an 'I.' But at the same time the 'I' seems to be a Nothing, the hypostasis of a pure form, something like an imagined substance" (Bachmann 1982: 42). Bachmann claims that poets are precisely those who "make the 'I' into the ground of their experiments, or who have made themselves into the experimental ground of the 'I'" (*ibid.*). This is why they "continually run the risk of going mad" (*ibid.*) and not knowing what they say.

But the idea of a fully desubjectified experience in the act of speech is also not foreign to the religious tradition. Many centuries before being programmatically taken up by Rimbaud in his letter to P. Demeny ("for 'I' is another. If brass wakes up a trumpet, it's not its fault"), a similar experience appeared as the common practice of a messianic community in Paul's first Letter to the Corinthians. The "speaking in tongues" (*lalein glōssē*) of which Paul writes refers to an event of speech — glossolalia — in which the speaker speaks without knowing what he says ("no man understandeth him; howbeit in the spirit he speaketh mysteries" [1 Corinthians 14:2]). Yet this means that the very principle of speech becomes something alien and "barbaric": "If I know not the meaning of the voice, I shall be unto him that speaketh a barbarian, and he that speaketh shall be a barbarian unto me" (14:11). The literal meaning of the term *barbaros*, a "barbarian," is a being not gifted with *logos*, a foreigner who does not truly know how to understand and speak. Glossolalia thus presents the aporia of an absolute desubjectification and "barbarization" of the event of language, in which the speaking subject gives way to another subject, a child, angel, or barbarian, who speaks "unfruitfully" and "into the air." And it is significant that although he does not altogether exclude the Corinthians' glossolalic practice, Paul alerts them to the puerile regression it implies, enjoining them to interpret what they say: "For if the trumpet give an uncertain sound, who shall prepare himself to the battle?... So likewise ye, except ye utter by the tongue words easy to be understood, how shall it be known what is spoken? For ye shall speak into the air.... Wherefore let him that speaketh in an unknown tongue pray that he may not interpret. For if I pray in an unknown tongue, my spirit prayeth, but my understanding is unfruitful.... Brethren, be not children in understanding" (14: 8–20).

3.15   The experience of glossolalia merely radicalizes a desubjectifying experience implicit in the simplest act of speech. Modern linguistic theory maintains that language and actual discourse are two absolutely divided orders, between which there can be neither transition nor communication. Saussure already observed that if language (in the sense of *langue*) in itself is constituted by a series of signs (for example, "mud," "lake," "sky," "red," "sad," "five," "to split," "to see"), nevertheless nothing makes it possible to foresee and understand how these signs will be put into action to form discourse. "The series of these words, as rich as it is through the ideas that it evokes, will never show one individual that another individual, in pronouncing them, means something." "The world of signs," Benveniste added a few years later, taking up and developing Saussure's antinomy, "is closed. From the sign to the phrase there is no transition, be it by syntagmatization or by any other means. A hiatus separates them" (Benveniste 1974: 65).

However, every language has at its disposal a series of signs (which linguistics call "shifters" or indicators of enunciation, among which, for example, there are the pronouns "I," "you," "this," and the adverbs "here," "now," etc.) destined to allow the individual to appropriate language in order to use it. Unlike other words, these signs do not possess a lexical meaning that can be defined in real terms; their meaning arises only through reference to the event of discourse in which they are used. "What then,"

Benveniste asks, "is the reality to which *I* or *you* refers? It is solely to a 'reality of discourse,' and this is a very strange thing. *I* cannot be defined except in terms of 'locution,' not in terms of objects as a nominal sign is. *I* signifies 'the person who is uttering the present instance of the discourse containing *I*'" (Benveniste 1971: 218).

Enunciation thus refers not to the *text* of what is stated, but to its *taking place*; the individual can put language into act only on condition of identifying himself with the very event of saying, and not with what is said in it. But then what does it mean "to appropriate language"? How is it possible to "start to speak" in these conditions?

When one looks closely, the passage from language to discourse appears as a paradoxical act that simultaneously implies both subjectification and desubjectification. On the one hand, the psychosomatic individual must fully abolish himself and desubjectify himself as a real individual to become the subject of enunciation and to identify himself with the pure shifter "I," which is absolutely without any substantiality and content other than its mere reference to the event of discourse. But, once stripped of all extra-linguistic meaning and constituted as a subject of enunciation, the subject discovers that he has gained access not so much to a possibility of speaking as to an impossibility of speaking — or, rather, that he has gained access to being always already anticipated by a glossolalic potentiality over which he has neither control nor mastery. Appropriating the formal instruments of enunciation, he is introduced into a language from which, by definition, nothing will allow him to pass into discourse. And yet, in saying "I," "you," "this," "now ... ," he is expropriated of all referential reality, letting himself be defined solely through the pure and empty relation to the event of discourse. *The subject of enunciation is composed of discourse and exists in discourse alone. But, for*

116

this very reason, once the subject is in discourse, he can say nothing; he cannot speak.

"I speak" is therefore just as contradictory a statement as is "I am a poet." For not only is the "I" always already *other* with respect to the individual who lends it speech; it does not even make sense to say that this *I-other* speaks, for insofar as it is solely sustained in a pure event of language, independent of every meaning, this *I-other* stands in an impossibility of speaking — he has nothing to say. In the absolute present of the event of discourse, subjectification and desubjectification coincide at every point, and both the flesh and blood individual and the subject of enunciation are perfectly silent. This can also be expressed by saying that the one who speaks is not the individual, but language; but this means nothing other than that an impossibility of speaking has, in an unknown way, come to speech.

It is therefore not surprising that in the face of this intimate extraneousness implicit in the act of speech, poets experience something like responsibility and shame. This is why Dante, in his *Vita nuova*, commanded the poet to know how "to open by prose" (*aprire per prosa*) the reasons of his poetry on pain of the "greatest shame." And it is difficult to forget the words with which Rimbaud evoked his earlier years as a poet: "I could not continue; I would have gone mad and, what is more...it was evil."

3.16   In twentieth-century poetry, Pessoa's letter on heteronyms constitutes perhaps the most impressive document of desubjectification, the transformation of the poet into a pure "experimentation ground," and its possible implications for ethics. On January 13, 1935, he responds to his friend Adolfo Casais Monteiro, who had asked him about the origin of his many heteronyms. He begins by presenting them as "an organic and constant tendency toward depersonalization:"

117

The origin of my heteronyms is basically an aspect of hysteria that exists within me. I don't know whether I am simply a hysteric or if I am more properly a neurasthenic hysteric. I tend toward the second hypothesis, because there are in me evidences of lassitude that hysteria, properly speaking, doesn't encompass in the list of its symptoms. Be that as it may, the mental origin of heteronyms lies in a persistent and organic tendency of mine to depersonalization and simulation. These phenomena — fortunately for me and others — intellectualize themselves. I mean, they don't show up in my practical life, on the surface and in contact with others; they explode inside, and I live with them alone in me.... An urging of spirit came upon me, absolutely foreign, for one reason or another, of that which I am, or which I suppose that I am. I spoke to it, immediately, spontaneously, as if it were a certain friend of mine whose name I invented, whose history I adapted, and whose figure — face, build, clothes, and manner — I immediately saw inside of me. And so I contrived and procreated various friends and acquaintances who never existed but whom still today — nearly thirty years later — I hear, feel, see. I repeat: I hear, feel, see.... And get greetings from them... (Pessoa 1988: 7–9).

Next comes the summary of the sudden personalization, on March 8, 1914, of one of his most memorable heteronyms, Alberto Caeiro, who was to become his teacher (or, rather, the teacher of another one of his heteronyms, Alvaro Do Campos):

I went over to a high desk and, taking a piece of paper, began to write, standing up, as I always do when I can. And I wrote some thirty poems, one after another, in a kind of ecstasy, the nature of which I am unable to define. It was the triumphant day of my life, and never will I have another like it. I began with the title, *The Keeper of Sheep*. What followed was the appearance of someone in

118

me whom I named, from then on, Alberto Caeiro. Forgive me the absurdity of the sentence: In me there appeared my master. That was my immediate reaction. So much so that scarcely were those thirty-odd poems written when I snatched more paper and wrote, again without stopping, the six poems constituting "Oblique Rain," by Fernando Pessoa. Straight away and completely.... It was the return of Fernando Pessoa/Alberto Caeiro to Fernando Pessoa himself. Or better, it was the reaction of Fernando Pessoa against his nonexistence as Alberto Caeiro (*ibid.*: 9).

It is worth examining this incomparable phenomenology of heteronymic depersonalization. Not only does each new subjectification (the appearance of Alberto Caeiro) imply a desubjectification (the depersonalization of Fernando Pessoa, who submits himself to his teacher). At the same time, each desubjectification also implies a resubjectification: the return of Fernando Pessoa, who reacts to his non-existence, that is, to his depersonalization in Alberto Caeiro. It is as if the poetic experience constituted a complex process that involved at least three subjects — or rather, three different subjectifications-desubjectifications, since it is no longer possible to speak of a subject in the strict sense. First of all there is the psychosomatic individual Fernando Pessoa, who approaches his desk on March 8, 1914 to write. With respect to this subject, the poetic act can only imply a radical desubjectification, which coincides with the subjectification of Alberto Caeiro. But a new poetic consciousness, something like a genuine *ēthos* of poetry, begins once Fernando Pessoa, having survived his own depersonalization, returns to a self who both is and is no longer the first subject. Then he understands that he must react to his non-existence as Alberto Caeiro, *that he must respond to his own desubjectification.*

3.17 Let us now reread the phenomenology of testimony in Primo Levi, the impossible dialectic between the survivor and the *Muselmann*, the pseudo-witness and the "complete witness," the human and the inhuman. Testimony appears here as a process that involves at least two subjects: the first, the survivor, who can speak but who has nothing interesting to say; and the second, who "has seen the Gorgon," who "has touched bottom," and therefore has much to say but cannot speak. Which of the two bears witness? *Who is the subject of testimony?*

At first it appears that it is the human, the survivor, who bears witness to the inhuman, the *Muselmann*. But if the survivor bears witness *for* the *Muselmann* — in the technical sense of "on behalf of" or "by proxy" ("we speak in their stead, by proxy") — then, according to the legal principle by which the acts of the delegated are imputed to the delegant, it is in some way the *Muselmann* who bears witness. But this means that the one who truly bears witness in the human is the inhuman; it means that the human is nothing other than the agent of the inhuman, the one who lends the inhuman a voice. Or, rather, that there is no one who claims the title of "witness" by right. To speak, to bear witness, is thus to enter into a vertiginous movement in which something sinks to the bottom, wholly desubjectified and silenced, and something subjectified speaks without truly having anything to say of its own ("I tell of things ... that I did not actually experience"). Testimony takes place where the speechless one makes the speaking one speak and where the one who speaks bears the impossibility of speaking in his own speech, such that the silent and the speaking, the inhuman and the human enter into a zone of indistinction in which it is impossible to establish the position of the subject, to identify the "imagined substance" of the "I" and, along with it, the true witness.

This can also be expressed by saying that *the subject of testi-*

mony is the one who bears witness to a desubjectification. But this expression holds only if it is not forgotten that "to bear witness to a desubjectification" can only mean there is no subject of testimony ("I repeat, we are not ... the true witnesses") and that every testimony is a field of forces incessantly traversed by currents of subjectification and desubjectification.

Here it is possible to gage the insufficiency of the two opposed theses that divide accounts of Auschwitz: the view of humanist discourse, which states that "all human beings are human" and that of anti-humanist discourse, which holds that "only some human beings are human." What testimony says is something completely different, which can be formulated in the following theses: "human beings are human insofar as they are not human" or, more precisely, "human beings are human insofar as they bear witness to the inhuman."

3.18   Let us consider the individual living being, the "infant" in the etymological sense, a being who cannot speak. What happens in him — and for him — in the moment he says "I" and begins to speak? We have seen that the "I," the subjectivity to which he gains access, is a purely discursive reality that refers neither to a concept nor to a real individual. The "I" that, as a unity transcending the multiple totality of lived experiences, guarantees the permanence of what we call consciousness is nothing other than the appearance in Being of an exclusively linguistic property. As Benveniste writes, "It is in the instance of discourse in which *I* designates the speaker that the speaker proclaims himself as the 'subject.' And so it is literally true that the basis of subjectivity is in the exercise of language" (Benveniste 1971: 226). Linguists have analyzed the consequences of the insertion of subjectivity into language for the structure of languages. The consequences of subjectification for the living individual, however, remain largely to be considered. It is thanks to this unprecedented self-presence as "I," as speaker in the event of discourse, that there can be in the living being something like a unitary center to which one can refer lived experiences and acts, a firm point outside of the oceans of sensations and psychic states. And Benveniste has shown how human temporality is generated through the self-presence and presence to the world that the act of enunciation makes possible, how human beings in general have no way to experience the "now" other than by constituting it through the insertion of discourse into the world in saying "I" and "now." But precisely for this reason, precisely because it has no other reality than discourse, the "now" — as shown by every attempt to grasp the present instant — is marked by an irreducible negativity; precisely because consciousness has no other consistency than language, everything that philosophy and psychology believed themselves to discern in consciousness is simply a shadow of language, an "imagined substance." Subjectivity and consciousness, in which our culture believed itself to have found its firmest foundation, rest on what is most precarious and fragile in the world: the event of speech. But this unsteady foundation reaffirms itself — and sinks away once again — every time we put language into action in discourse, in the most frivolous chatter as in speech given once and for all to oneself and to others.

There is more: the living being who has made himself absolutely present to himself in the act of enunciation, in saying "I," pushes his own lived experiences back into a limitless past and can no longer coincide with them. The event of language in the pure presence of discourse irreparably divides the self-presence of sensations and experiences in the very moment in which it refers them to a unitary center. Whoever enjoys the particular presence achieved in the intimate consciousness of the enunciating voice forever loses the pristine adhesion to the Open that Rilke dis-

SHAME, OR ON THE SUBJECT

cerned in the gaze of the animal; he must now turn his eyes inward toward the non-place of language. This is why subjectification, the production of consciousness in the event of discourse, is often a trauma of which human beings are not easily cured; this is why the fragile text of consciousness incessantly crumbles and erases itself, bringing to light the disjunction on which it is erected: the constitutive desubjectification in every subjectification. (It is hardly astonishing that it was precisely from an analysis of the pronoun "I" in Husserl that Derrida was able to draw his idea of an infinite deferral, an originary disjunction – writing – inscribed in the pure self-presence of consciousness.)

It is therefore not surprising that when something like consciousness (*suneidēsis, sunnoia*) makes its appearance in the work of Greek tragedians and poets, it appears as the inscription of a zone of non-consciousness in language and of silence in knowledge, which has an ethical rather than logical connotation from the beginning. Thus in Solon's *Eunomia*, Dikē has the form of a mute con-science (*sigōsa sunoide*), and for the tragedians consciousness can also be attributed to an inanimate object which, by definition, cannot speak: the sleepless bed in *Electra* and the rocky cavern in *Philoctetus* (cf. Agamben 1991: 91). When a subject appears for the first time as a consciousness, it thus has the form of a disjunction between knowing and saying. For the one who knows, it is felt as an impossibility of speaking; for the one who speaks, it is experienced as an equally bitter impossibility to know.

3.19   In 1928, Ludwig Binswanger published a study bearing the significant title *The Vital Function and Internal History of Life*. Introducing into psychiatric terminology a phenomenological vocabulary that is still imprecise, Binswanger develops the idea of a fundamental heterogeneity between the plane of the physical and psychical vital functions that take place in an organism and in personal consciousness, in which the lived experiences of an individual are organized into an inner unitary history. In the place of the old distinction between the psychic and the somatic, Binswanger proposes the much more decisive distinction between the "functional modality of the psycho-somatic organism, on the one hand, and the internal history of life on the other." This allows him to escape the confusion "between the concept of psychic function and the spiritual content of psychic lived experiences," which is both "inherent in the psychic term and by now scientifically unsound."

In a later work (which Foucault commented on), Binswanger compares this duality to the opposition between dreaming and waking. "Dreaming, man — to use a distinction I have drawn elsewhere — is 'life-function;' waking, he creates 'life history.' ... It is not possible — no matter how the attempt is made — to reduce both parts of the disjunction between life-function and life-history to a common denominator, because life considered as function is not the same as life considered as history" (Binswanger 1963: 247–48).

Binswanger limits himself to noting this opposition and to suggesting that the psychiatrist ought to take account of both points of view. But he indicates an aporia so radical that the very possibility of identifying a unitary terrain of consciousness is called into question. Consider, on the one hand, the continuous flow of vital functions: respiration, circulation, digestion, homeothermy (but also sensation, muscular movement, irritation, etc.) and, on the other hand, the flow of language and of the conscious "I," in which lived experiences are organized into an individual history. Is there a point in which these two flows are unified, in which the "dreaming" of the vital functions is joined to the "waking" of personal consciousness? Where, and how, can a subject be introduced into the biological flow? Is it possible to say that at the point in which the speaker, saying "I," is produced as a subject, there is something like a coincidence between these two series, in which the speaking subject can truly assume his own biological functions as his own, in which the living being can identify himself with the speaking and thinking "I"? In the cyclical development of bodily processes as in the series of consciousness' intentional acts, nothing seems to consent to such a coincidence. Indeed, "I" signifies precisely the irreducible disjunction between vital functions and inner history, between the living being's becoming a speaking being and the speaking being's sensation of itself as living. It is certainly true that the two series flow alongside one another in what one could call absolute intimacy. But is *intimacy* not precisely the name that we give to a proximity that also remains distant, to a promiscuity that never becomes identity?

3.20   The Japanese psychiatrist Kimura Bin, director of the Psychiatric Hospital of Kyoto and translator of Binswanger, sought to deepen Heidegger's analysis of temporality in *Being and Time* with reference to a classification of the fundamental types of mental illness. To this end he made use of the Latin formula *post festum* (literally, "after the celebration"), which indicates an irreparable past, an arrival at things that are already done. *Post festum* is symmetrically distinguished from *ante festum* ("before the celebration") and *intra festum* ("during the celebration").

Post festum temporality is that of the melancholic, who always experiences his own "I" in the form of an "I was," of an irrecoverably accomplished past with respect to which one can only be in debt. This experience of time corresponds in Heidegger to *Dasein*'s Being-thrown, its finding itself always already abandoned to a factual situation beyond which it can never venture. There is thus a kind of constitutive "melancholy" of human *Dasein*, which is always late with respect to itself, having always already missed its "celebration."

Ante festum temporality corresponds to the experience of the schizophrenic, in which the direction of the melancholic's orientation toward the past is inverted. For the schizophrenic, the "I" is never a certain possession; it is always something to be attained, and the schizophrenic therefore always lives time in the form of anticipation. "The 'I' of the schizophrenic," Kimura Bin writes, "is not the 'I' of the 'already been'; it is not tied to a duty. In other words, it is not the *post festum* 'I' of the melancholic, which can only be spoken of in terms of a past and a debt.... Instead, the essential point here is the problem of one's own possibility of being oneself, the problem of the certainty of becoming oneself and, therefore, the risk of possibly being alienated from oneself" (Kimura Bin 1992: 79). In *Being and Time*, the schizophrenic's temporality corresponds to the primacy of the future in the form of projection and anticipation. Precisely because its experience of time originally temporalizes itself on the basis of the future, *Dasein* can be defined by Heidegger as "the being for whom, in its very Being, Being is always at issue" and also as "in its Being always already anticipating itself." But precisely for this reason, *Dasein* is constitutively schizophrenic; it always risks missing itself and not being present at its own "celebration."

One might expect the temporal dimension of *intra festum* to correspond to a point between the melancholic's irreparable self-loss and the schizophrenic's advance absence at his own ceremony, a point in which human beings would finally gain access to a full self-presence, finding their *dies festus*. But it is not so. The two examples of *intra festum* Kimura Bin provides have nothing celebratory about them. In the first case, obsessive neurosis, the adherence to the present takes the form of an obsessive reiteration of the same act with the intention, so to speak, of procuring proof of being oneself, of not always having missed oneself. In other words, the obsessive type seeks through repetition to document his own presence at a celebration that constantly eludes him. The constitutive self-loss characteristic of *intra festum* temporality is even clearer in Kimura Bin's second example: epilepsy, which he presents as the "original landscape" of insanity — a particular form of self-loss achieved through a kind of ecstatic excess over presence. According to Kimura Bin, the decisive question for epilepsy is: "Why does the epileptic lose consciousness?" His answer is that in the point in which the "I" is about to adhere to itself in the supreme moment of celebration, the epileptic crisis confirms consciousness' incapacity to tolerate presence, to participate at its own celebration. In Dostoevsky's words, which he cites at this point: "There are instants that last no longer than five or six seconds, in which all of a sudden you hear the presence of eternal harmony, and in which you have reached it. It is not earthly. But I do not want to say that it is heavenly either; only that in his earthly form man is incapable of tolerating it. He must either be physically transformed or die" (*ibid.*: 151).

Kimura Bin does not offer an example of epileptic temporality in *Being and Time*. And yet it is possible to suppose that it concerns the instant of decision, in which anticipation and having been, schizophrenic temporality and melancholic temporality coincide, and the "I" comes to itself in authentically assuming its own irreparable past ("its anticipation of its most extreme and ownmost possibility is a return to its own having been"). The silent and anguished decision that anticipates and assumes its own end would then be something like *Dasein*'s epileptic aura, in which *Dasein* "touches the world of death in the form of an excess, an excess that is both an overflowing and a source of life" (*ibid.*: 152). In any case, according to Kimura Bin, man seems necessarily to dwell in a disjunction with respect to himself and his own *dies festus*. Almost as if living beings were constitutively divided on account of having become speaking beings, of having said 'I,' and as if time were nothing other than the form of this disjunction. And as if this disjunction could be mastered only in the epileptic excess or the moment of authentic decision, which represent something like the invisible architraves sustaining the ecstatico-horizontal edifice of time, keeping it from caving in on Being-There's spatial situation, its There.

From this perspective, Auschwitz marks the irrecoverable crisis of authentic temporality, of the very possibility of "deciding" on the disjunction. The camp, the absolute situation, is the end of every possibility of an originary temporality, that is, of the temporal foundation of a singular position in space, of a *Da*. In the camp, the irreparability of the past takes the form of an absolute imminence; *post festum* and *ante festum*, anticipation and succession are parodically flattened on each other. Waking is now forever drawn into the inside of the dream: "Soon we will again hear / the foreign command: / *Wstawac!*"

3.21   It is now possible to clarify the sense in which shame is truly something like the hidden structure of all subjectivity and consciousness. Insofar as it consists solely in the event of enunciation, consciousness constitutively has the form of being consigned to something that cannot be assumed. To be conscious means: to be consigned to something that cannot be assumed. (Hence both guilt as the structure of conscience in Heidegger and the necessity of the unconscious in Freud.)

Consider the old philosophical definition of man as *zōon logon echōn*, the living being who has language. The metaphysical tradition has interrogated this definition with regard both to the living being and to *logos*. And yet what has remained unthought in it is the *echōn*, the mode of this having. How can a living being *have* language? What can it mean for a living being to speak?

The preceding analyses have sufficiently shown the sense in which speaking is a paradoxical act that implies both subjectification and desubjectification, in which the living individual appropriates language in a full expropriation alone, becoming a speaking being only on condition of falling into silence. The mode of Being of this "I," the existential status of the speaking-living-being is thus a kind of ontological glossolalia, an absolutely insubstantial chatter in which the living being and the speaking being, subjectification and desubjectification, can never coincide. This is why metaphysics and the Western reflection on language — if they are two different things — have constantly sought to articulate the relation between the living being and the speaking being, to construct a link securing communication between what seems incommunicable, giving consistency to the "imagined substance" of the subject and its ungraspable glossolalia.

This is not the place to show how this articulation has been generally sought in the site of an "I" or a Voice — as a silent voice of conscience that appears to itself in inner discourse, on the one hand, and on the other, as an articulated voice, *phōnē enarthos*, in which language is securely joined to the living being by being inscribed in its very voice. And yet in the final analysis this Voice is always a mythologeme or a *theologoumenon*; nowhere, in the living being or in language, can we reach a point in which something like an articulation truly takes place. Outside theology and the incarnation of the Verb, there is no moment in which language is inscribed in the living voice, no place in which the living being is able to render itself linguistic, transforming itself into speech.

It is in this non-place of articulation that deconstruction inscribes its "trace" and its *différance*, in which voice and letter, meaning and presence are infinitely differed. The line that, in Kant, marked the only possible way to represent the auto-affection of time is now the movement of a writing on which "the 'look' cannot 'abide'" (Derrida 1973: 104). But precisely this impossibility of conjoining the living being and language, *phōnē* and *logos*, the inhuman and the human — far from authorizing the infinite deferral of signification — is what allows for testimony. If there is no articulation between the living being and language, if the "I" stands suspended in this disjunction, then there can be testimony. The intimacy that betrays our non-coincidence with ourselves is the place of testimony. *Testimony takes place in the non-place of articulation.* In the non-place of the Voice stands not writing, but the witness. And it is precisely because the relation (or, rather, non-relation) between the living being and the speaking being has the form of shame, of being reciprocally consigned to something that cannot be assumed by a subject, that the *ēthos* of this disjunction can only be testimony — that is, something that cannot be assigned to a subject but that nevertheless constitutes the subject's only dwelling place, its only possible consistency.

3.22   Giorgio Manganelli has written of a special figure of heteronymy, which he calls "pseudonymy squared" or "homopseudonymy." It consists in using a pseudonym that is in every respect identical to one's own name. One day, one of his friends tells him that he has published a book of which he knows nothing, just as other times it had also happened to him that "sober-minded people" let him know they have seen books with his first and last name on display in credible bookstore windows. $(Pseudonymy)^2$ brings the paradox of ontological heteronymy to an extreme point, since here it is not only an "I" that gives way to another; this "other" even claims not to be "other," but rather fully identical to the "I," something the "I" cannot but deny. "I had acquired and partially read a book that an honest slanderer, an historicist, a specialist of anagraphs had called 'mine.' But if I had written it, if there had been an 'I' capable of writing a book, that book, what could explain the absolute, irritating strangeness that divided me from what had been written?" (Manganelli 1996: 13).

With respect to the simple "I," the homopseudonym is absolutely foreign and perfectly intimate, both unconditionally real and necessarily non-existent, so much so that no language could describe it; no text could guarantee its consistency. "So I had written nothing. But by 'I' I meant the person with my name and without pseudonym. Did the pseudonym write? It's likely, but the pseudonym pseudowrites; it is technically speaking unreadable by the 'I,' although it might be readable by the squared pseudonym 'I,' who obviously does not exist. But if the reader is non-existent, I know what he can read: what can be written by the degree zero pseudonym, something that cannot be read by anyone who is not the squared pseudonym, the non-existent one. In fact, what is written is nothing. The book means nothing, and in any case I cannot read it without giving up my existence. Maybe it's all a prank: as will be made clear, I have been dead now for many years, like the friend I met, and the book I'm leafing through is always incomprehensible; I read it, I reread it, I lose it. Maybe one has to die several times" (*ibid.*: 14).

What this terribly serious joke lays bare is nothing less than the ontological paradox of the living-speaking (or writing)-being, the living being who can say "I." As a simple "I" with a name but no pseudonym, he can neither write nor say anything. But every proper name, insofar as it names a living being, a non-linguistic thing, is always a pseudonym (a "degree zero pseudonym"). I can only write and speak as the pseudonym "I"; but what I then write and say is nothing, that is something that could be read or heard only by a squared pseudonym, who does not exist in himself, if not by taking the place of the first "I," who then gives up his existence (that is, dies). At this point, the pseudonym's elevation to the second power is complete: the "I" with a name but no pseudonym disappears in the non-existent homopseudonym.

But the next question is: Who is speaking in Manganelli's story, who is its author? Who bears witness to the unease of this intimate strangeness? The "I" without pseudonym, which exists but cannot write? Or the degree zero pseudonym, who writes the unreadable text of the first "I"? Or rather the third, the squared pseudonym who reads, rereads, and loses the empty and incomprehensible book? If it is clear that "I have been dead for many years," who survives to speak of this death? In the process of vertiginous, heteronymic subjectification, it is as if something always survived, as if a final or residual "I" were generated in the word "I," such that the pseudonym's elevation to the second power were never truly completed, as if the squared "I" always fell back onto a new "I," an "I" both indistinguishable from and irreducible to the first.

3.23   The term "to survive" contains an ambiguity that cannot be eliminated. It implies the reference to something or someone that is survived. The Latin *supervivo* — like the equivalent *superstes sum* — is in this sense constructed with the dative, to indicate the person or thing with respect to which there is survival. But from the beginning, the verb also has a reflexive form when referred to human beings, which designates the striking idea of survival with respect to oneself and one's own life. In this form, the one who survives and the person to whom something survives thus coincide. If Pliny can therefore say of a public figure that "for thirty years he had survived his glory" (*triginta annis gloriae suae supervixit*), in Apuleius we already find the idea of genuine posthumous existence, a life that lives by surviving itself (*etiam mihi ipse*

132

supervivens et postumus). In the same sense, Christian authors can say that Christ — and every Christian along with him — is both testator and inheritor insofar as he has survived death (*Christus idem testator et haeres, qui morti propriae supervivit*); moreover, they also can write that the sinner survives on earth on account of being in truth spiritually dead (*animam tuam misera perdidisti, spiritualiter mortua supervivere hic tibi*).

This implies that in human beings, life bears with it a caesura that can transform all life into survival and all survival into life. In a sense — the sense we have encountered in Bettelheim — survival designates the pure and simple continuation of bare life with respect to truer and more human life. In another sense, survival has a positive sense and refers — as in Des Pres — to the person who, in fighting against death, has survived the inhuman.

Let us then formulate the thesis that summarizes the lesson of Auschwitz: *The human being is the one who can survive the human being.* In the first sense, it refers to the *Muselmann* (or the gray zone); it therefore signifies the inhuman capacity to survive the human. In the second sense, it refers to the survivor; it designates the human being's capacity to survive the *Muselmann*, the nonhuman. When one looks closely, however, the two senses converge in one point, which can be said to constitute their most intimate semantic core, in which the two meanings momentarily seem to coincide. The *Muselmann* stands in this point; and it is in him that we find the third, truest, and most ambiguous sense of the thesis, which Levi proclaims when he writes that "they, the *Muselmän-ner*, the drowned are the complete witnesses": *the human being is the inhuman; the one whose humanity is completely destroyed is the one who is truly human.* The paradox here is that if the only one bearing witness to the human is the one whose humanity has been wholly destroyed, this means that the identity between human and inhuman is never perfect and that it is not truly possible to

133

destroy the human, that something always *remains. The witness is this remnant.*

3.24   Concerning Antelme's book, Blanchot once wrote that "man is the indestructible that can be infinitely destroyed" (Blanchot 1993: 130). The word "indestructible" here does not mean something — an essence or human relation — that infinitely resists its own infinite destruction. Blanchot misunderstands his own words when he sees infinite destruction as the place of "the human relation in its primacy," as the relation to the Other (*ibid.*: 135). The indestructible does not exist, either as essence or as relation; Blanchot's sentence must be read in another sense, one that is both more complicated and simpler. "Man is the indestructible who can be infinitely destroyed" — like "the human being is the one who can survive the human being" — is not a definition which, like all good logical definitions, identifies a human essence in attributing a specific difference to it. The human being can survive the human being, the human being is what remains after the destruction of the human being, not because somewhere there is a human essence to be destroyed or saved, but because the place of the human is divided, because the human being exists in the fracture between the living being and the speaking being, the inhuman and the human. That is: *the human being exists in the human being's non-place, in the missing articulation between the living being and logos.* The human being is the being that is lacking to itself and that consists solely in this lack and in the errancy it opens. When Grete Salus wrote that "man should never have to bear everything that he can bear, nor should he ever have to see how this suffering to the most extreme power no longer has anything human about it," she also meant this much: there is no human essence; the human being is a potential being and, in the moment in which human beings think they have grasped the essence of the human in its infinite destructibility, what then appears is something that "no longer has anything human about it."

The human being is thus always beyond or before the human, the central threshold through which pass currents of the human and the inhuman, subjectification and desubjectification, the living being's becoming speaking and the logos' becoming living. These currents are coextensive, but not coincident; their non-coincidence, the subtle ridge that divides them, is the place of testimony.

CHAPTER FOUR

The Archive and Testimony

4.1   One evening in 1969, Emile Benveniste, Professor of Linguistics at the Collège de France, suffered an attack on a street in Paris. Without identification papers, he was not recognized. By the time he was identified, he had already suffered a complete and incurable aphasia that lasted until his death in 1972 and kept him from working in any way. In 1972, the journal *Semiotica* published his essay, "The Semiology of Language." At the end of this article, Benveniste outlines a research program that moves beyond Saussurian linguistics, one that was never realized. It is not surprising that the basis for this program lies in the theory of enunciation, which may well constitute Benveniste's most felicitous creation. The overcoming of Saussurian linguistics, he argues, is to be accomplished in two ways: the first, which is perfectly comprehensible, is by a semantics of discourse distinct from the theory of signification founded on the paradigm of the sign; the second, which interests us here, consists instead "in the translinguistic analysis of texts and works through the elaboration of a metasemantics that will be constructed on the basis of a semantics of enunciation" (Benveniste 1974: 65).

It is necessary to linger on the aporia implicit in this formulation. If enunciation, as we know, does not refer to the text of what is uttered but to its taking place, if it is nothing other than language's pure reference to itself as actual discourse, in what sense is it possible to speak of a "semantics" of enunciation? To be sure, the isolation of the domain of enunciation first makes it possible to distinguish in a statement between what is said and its taking place. But does enunciation not then represent a non-semantic dimension precisely on account of this identification? It is certainly possible to define something like a meaning of the shifters "I," "you," "now," "here" (for example, "'I' means the one who utters the present speech in which 'I' is contained"); but this meaning is completely foreign to the lexical meaning of other linguistic signs. "I" is neither a notion nor a substance, and enunciation concerns not what is said in discourse but the pure fact that it is said, the event of language as such, which is by definition ephemeral. Like the philosophers' concept of Being, enunciation is what is most unique and concrete, since it refers to the absolutely singular and unrepeatable event of discourse in act; but at the same time, it is what is most vacuous and generic, since it is always repeated without its ever being possible to assign it any lexical reality.

What, from this perspective, can it mean to speak of a metasemantics founded on a semantics of enunciation? What did Benveniste glimpse before falling into aphasia?

4.2   In 1969, Michel Foucault also publishes *The Archaeology of Knowledge*, which formulates the method and program of his research through the foundation of a theory of statements (*énoncés*). Although Benveniste's name does not appear in the book and despite the fact that Foucault could not have known Benveniste's last articles, a secret thread ties Foucault's program to the one the linguist outlined. The incomparable novelty of *The Archaeology of Knowledge* consists in having explicitly taken as its object neither sentences nor propositions but precisely "statements," that is, not the text of discourse but its taking place. Foucault was thus the first to comprehend the novel dimension of Benveniste's theory of enunciation, and he was the first then to make this dimension into an object of study. Foucault certainly recognized that this object is, in a certain sense, undefinable, that archaeology in no way delimits a particular linguistic area comparable to those assigned to the various disciplines of knowledge. Insofar as enunciation refers not to a text but to a pure event of language (in the terms of the Stoics, not to something said but to the sayable that remains unsaid in it), its territory cannot coincide with a definite level of linguistic analysis (the sentence, the proposition, illocutive acts, etc.), or with the specific domains examined by the sciences. Instead, it represents a function vertically present in all sciences and in all acts of speech. As Foucault writes, with lucid awareness of his method's ontological implications: "the statement is not therefore a structure . . . ; it is a function of existence" (Foucault 1972: 86). In other words: enunciation is not a thing determined by real, definite properties; it is, rather, pure existence, the fact that a certain being — language — takes place. Given the system of the sciences and the many knowledges that, inside language, define meaningful sentences and more or less well formed discourses, archaeology claims as its territory the pure taking place of these propositions and discourses, that is, the *outside* of language, the brute fact of its existence.

In this way, Foucault's archaeology perfectly realizes Benveniste's program for a "metasemantics built on a semantics of enunciation." After having used a semantics of enunciation to distinguish the domain of statements from that of propositions, Foucault establishes a new point of view from which to investigate knowledges and disciplines, an *outside* that makes it possible to reconsider the field of disciplinary discourses through a "meta-semantics": archaeology.

It is certainly possible that Foucault thus merely dressed up old ontology, which had become unacceptable, in the modern garb of a new historical metadiscipline, thereby ironically proposing first philosophy not as a knowledge, but as an "archaeology" of all knowledges. But such an interpretation fails to recognize the novelty of Foucault's method. What gives his inquiry its incomparable efficiency is its refusal to grasp the taking place of language through an "I," a transcendental consciousness or, worse, an equally mythological psychosomatic "I." Instead, Foucault decisively poses the question of how something like a subject, an "I," or a consciousness can correspond to statements, to the pure taking place of language.

Insofar as the human sciences define themselves by establishing a linguistic stratum that corresponds to a certain level of meaningful discourse and linguistic analysis (the sentence, the proposition, the illocutive act, etc.), their subject is naively identified with the psychosomatic individual presumed to utter discourse. On the other hand, modern philosophy, which strips the transcendental subject of its anthropological and psychological attributes, reducing it to a pure "I speak," is not fully aware of the transformation this reduction implies with respect to the experience of language; it does not recognize the fact that language is thereby displaced onto an asemantic level that can no longer be that of propositions. In truth, to take seriously the statement "I speak" is no longer to consider language as the communication of a meaning or a truth that originates in a responsible Subject. It is, rather, to conceive of discourse in its pure taking place and of the subject as "a nonexistence in whose emptiness the unending outpouring of language uninterruptedly continues" (Foucault 1998: 148). In language, enunciation marks a threshold between an inside and an outside, its taking place as pure exteriority; and once the principal referent of study becomes statements, the subject is stripped of all substance, becoming a pure function or pure position. The subject, Foucault writes, "is a particular, vacant place that may in fact be filled by different individuals.... If a proposition, a sentence, a group of signs can be called 'statement,' it is not therefore because, one day, someone happened to speak them or put them into some concrete form of writing; it is because the position of the subject can be assigned. To describe a formulation *qua* statement does not consist in analyzing the relations between the author and what he says (or wanted to say, or said without wanting to); but in determining what position can and must be occupied by any individual if he is to be the subject of it" (Foucault 1972: 95–6).

In the same year, Foucault undertakes his critique of the notion of the author following these very same principles. His interest is not so much to note the author's eclipse or to certify his death as to define the concept of the author as a simple specification of the subject-function whose necessity is anything but given: "We can easily imagine a culture where discourse would circulate without any need for an author. Discourses, whatever their status, form or value, and regardless of our manner of handling them, would unfold in the anonymity of a murmur" (Foucault 1998: 222, translation emended).

4.3   In his understandable concern to define archeology's terrain with respect to other knowledges and domains, Foucault appears to have neglected — at least to a certain point — to consider the ethical implications of his theory of statements. Only in his last works, after having effaced and depsychologized the author, after having identified something like an ethics immanent to writing already in the bracketing of the question "Who is speaking?," did

Foucault begin to reflect on the consequences that his desubjectification and decomposition of the author implied for the subject. It is thus possible to say, in Benveniste's terms, that the
metasemantics of disciplinary discourses ended by concealing the
semantics of enunciation that had made it possible, and that the
constitution of the system of statements as a positivity and historical a priori made it necessary to forget the erasure of the subject
that was its presupposition. In this way, the just concern to do
away with the false question "Who is speaking?" hindered the formulation of an entirely different and inevitable question: What
happens in the living individual when he occupies the 'vacant
place' of the subject, when he enters into a process of enunciation and discovers that "our reason is the difference of discourses,
our history the difference of times, ourselves the difference of
masks?" (Foucault 1972: 131). That is, once again, what does it
mean to be subject to desubjectification? How can a subject give
an account of its own ruin?

This omission — if it is an omission — obviously does not correspond to a forgetfulness or an incapacity on Foucault's part; it
involves a difficulty implicit in the very concept of a semantics of
enunciation. Insofar as it inheres not in the text of the statement,
but rather in its taking place — insofar as it concerns not something said, but a pure saying — a semantics of enunciation cannot
constitute either a text or a discipline. The subject of enunciation, whose dispersion founds the possibility of a metasemantics
of knowledges and constitutes statements in a positive system,
maintains itself not in a content of meaning but in an event of
language; this is why it cannot take itself as an object, stating
itself. There can thus be no archaeology of the subject in the
sense in which there is an archaeology of knowledges.

Does this mean that the one who occupies the vacant place of
the subject is destined to be forever obscured and that the author

142

must lose himself fully in the anonymous murmur of "What does it matter who is speaking"? In Foucault's work, there is perhaps only one text in which this difficulty thematically comes to light, in which the darkness of the subject momentarily appears in all its splendor. This text is "The Life of Infamous Men," which was originally conceived as a preface to an anthology of archival documents, registers of internment or *lettres de cachet*. In the very moment in which it marks them with infamy, the encounter with power reveals human existences that would otherwise have left no traces of themselves. What momentarily shines through these laconic statements are not the biographical events of personal histories, as suggested by the pathos-laden emphasis of a certain oral history, but rather the luminous trail of a different history. What suddenly comes to light is not the memory of an oppressed existence, but the silent flame of an immemorable *ēthos* — not the subject's face, but rather the disjunction between the living being and the speaking being that marks its empty place. Here life subsists only in the infamy in which it existed; here a name lives solely in the disgrace that covered it. And something in this disgrace bears witness to life beyond all biography.

4.4   Foucault gives the name "archive" to the positive dimension that corresponds to the plane of enunciation, "the general system of the formation and transformation of statements" (Foucault 1972: 130). How are we to conceive of this dimension, if it corresponds neither to the archive in the strict sense — that is, the storehouse that catalogs the traces of what has been said, to consign them to future memory — nor to the Babelic library that gathers the dust of statements and allows for their resurrection under the historian's gaze?

As the set of rules that define the events of discourse, the archive is situated between *langue*, as the system of construction

143

of possible sentences — that is, of possibilities of speaking — and the *corpus* that unites the set of what has been said, the things actually uttered or written. The archive is thus the mass of the non-semantic inscribed in every meaningful discourse as a function of its enunciation; it is the dark margin encircling and limiting every concrete act of speech. Between the obsessive memory of tradition, which knows only what has been said, and the exaggerated thoughtlessness of oblivion, which cares only for what was never said, the archive is the unsaid or sayable inscribed in everything said by virtue of being enunciated; it is the fragment of memory that is always forgotten in the act of saying "I." It is in this "historical a priori," suspended between *langue* and *parole*, that Foucault establishes his construction site and founds archaeology as "the general theme of a description that questions the already-said at the level of its existence" (*ibid.*: 131) — that is, as the system of relations between the unsaid and the said in every act of speech, between the enunciative function and the discourse in which it exerts itself, between the outside and the inside of language.

Let us now attempt to repeat Foucault's operation, sliding it toward language (*langue*), thus displacing the site that he had established between *langue* and the acts of speech, to relocate it in the difference between language (*langue*) and archive: that is, not between discourse and its taking place, between what is said and the enunciation that exerts itself in it, but rather between *langue* and its taking place, between a pure possibility of speaking and its existence as such. If enunciation in some way lies suspended between *langue* and *parole*, it will then be a matter of considering statements not from the point of view of actual discourse, but rather from that of language (*langue*); it will be a question of looking from the site of enunciation not toward an act of speech, but toward *langue* as such: that is, of articulating an inside and an outside not only in the plane of language and actual discourse, but also in the plane of language as potentiality of speech.

In opposition to the *archive*, which designates the system of relations between the unsaid and the said, we give the name *testimony* to the system of relations between the inside and the outside of *langue*, between the sayable and the unsayable in every language — that is, between a potentiality of speech and its existence, between a possibility and an impossibility of speech. To think a potentiality in act *as potentiality*, to think enunciation on the plane of *langue* is to inscribe a caesura in possibility, a caesura that divides it into a possibility and an impossibility, into a potentiality and an impotentiality; and it is to situate a subject in this very caesura. The archive's constitution presupposed the bracketing of the subject, who was reduced to a simple function or an empty position; it was founded on the subject's disappearance into the anonymous murmur of statements. In testimony, by contrast, the empty place of the subject becomes the decisive question. It is not a question, of course, of returning to the old problem that Foucault had sought to eliminate, namely, "How can a subject's freedom be inserted into the rules of a language?" Rather, it is a matter of situating the subject in the disjunction between a possibility and an impossibility of speech, asking, "How can something like a statement exist in the site of *langue*? In what way can a possibility of speech realize itself as such?" Precisely because testimony is the relation between a possibility of speech and its taking place, it can exist only through a relation to an impossibility of speech — that is, only as *contingency*, as a capacity not to be. This contingency, this occurrence of language in a subject, is different from actual discourse's utterance or non-utterance, its speaking or not speaking, its production or non-production as a statement. It concerns the subject's capacity to have or not to

145

have language. The subject is thus the possibility that language does not exist, does not take place — or, better, that it takes place only through its possibility of not being there, its contingency. The human being is the speaking being, the living being who has language, because the human being is capable of *not having* language, because it is capable of its own in-fancy. Contingency is not one modality among others, alongside possibility, impossibility, and necessity: it is the actual giving of a possibility, the way in which a potentiality exists as such. It is an event (*contingit*) of a potentiality as the giving of a caesura between a capacity to be and a capacity not to be. In language, this giving has the form of subjectivity. Contingency is possibility put to the test of a subject.

In the relation between what is said and its taking place, it was possible to bracket the subject of enunciation, since speech had already taken place. But the relation between language and its existence, between *langue* and the archive, demands subjectivity as that which, in its very possibility of speech, bears witness to an impossibility of speech. This is why subjectivity appears as *witness*; this is why it can speak for those who cannot speak. Testimony is a potentiality that becomes actual through an impotentiality of speech; it is, moreover, an impossibility that gives itself existence through a possibility of speaking. These two movements cannot be identified either with a subject or with a consciousness; yet they cannot be divided into two incommunicable substances. Their inseparable intimacy is testimony.

4.5   It is time to attempt to redefine the categories of modality from the perspective that interests us. The modal categories — possibility, impossibility, contingency, necessity — are not innocuous logical or epistemological categories that concern the structure of propositions or the relation of something to our faculty of knowledge. They are ontological operators, that is, the devastating weapons used in the biopolitical struggle for Being, in which a decision is made each time on the human and inhuman, on "making live" or "letting die." The field of this battle is subjectivity. The fact that Being gives itself in modalities means that "for living beings, Being is life" (*to de zēn tois zōsi einai estin*) (Aristotle, *De anima:* 413b13); it implies a living subject. The categories of modality are not founded on the subject, as Kant maintains, nor are they derived from it; rather, the subject is what is at stake in the processes in which they interact. They divide and separate, in the subject, what is possible and what is impossible, the living being and the speaking being, the *Muselmann* and the witness— and in this way they decide on the subject.

Possibility (to be able to be) and contingency (to be able not to be) are the operators of subjectivication, the point in which something possible passes into existence, giving itself through a relation to an impossibility. Impossibility, as negation of possibility (not [to be able]), and necessity, as negation of contingency (not [to be able not to be]) are the operators of desubjectification, of the destruction and destitution of the subject—that is, processes that, in subjectivity, divide potentiality and impotentiality, the possible and the impossible. The first two constitute Being in its subjectivity, that is, in the final analysis as a world that is always my world, since it is in my world that impossibility exists and touches (*contingit*) the real. Necessity and impossibility, instead, define Being in its wholeness and solidity, pure substantiality without subject—that is, at the limit, a world that is never *my* world since possibility does not exist in it. Yet modal catagories, as operators of Being, never stand before the subject as something he can choose or reject; and they do not confront him as a task that he can decide to assume or not to assume in a privileged moment. The subject, rather, is a field of forces always already traversed by the incandescent and historically determined currents of potentiality and impotentiality, of being able not to be and not being able not to be.

From this perspective, Auschwitz represents the historical point in which these processes collapse, the devastating experience in which the impossible is forced into the real. Auschwitz is the existence of the impossible, the most radical negation of contingency; it is, therefore, absolute necessity. The *Muselmann* produced by Auschwitz is the catastrophe of the subject that then follows, the subject's effacement as the place of contingency and its maintenance as existence of the impossible. Here Goebbel's definition of politics — "the art of making what seems impossible possible" — acquires its full weight. It defines a biopolitical experiment on the operators of Being, an experiment that transforms and disarticulates the subject to a limit point in which the link between subjectification and desubjectification seems to break apart.

4.6   The modern meaning of the term "author" appears relatively late. In Latin, *auctor* originally designates the person who intervenes in the case of a minor (or the person who, for whatever reason, does not have the capacity to posit a legally valid act), in order to grant him the valid title that he requires. Thus the tutor, uttering the formula *auctor fio*, furnishes the pupil with the "authority" he lacks (one then says that the pupil acts *tutore auctore*). In the same way, *auctoritas patrum* is the ratification that the senators — thus called *patres auctores* — bring to a popular resolution to make it valid and obligatory in all cases.

The oldest meanings of the term also include "vendor" in the act of transferring property, "he who advises or persuades" and, finally, "witness." In what way can a term that expressed the idea of the completion of an imperfect act also signify seller, adviser, and witness? What is the common character that lies at the root of these apparently heterogeneous meanings?

As to the meanings of "seller" and "adviser," a quick examination of the relevant texts suffices to confirm their substantial pertinence to the term's fundamental meaning. The seller is said to be *auctor* insofar as his will, merging with that of the buyer, validates and legitimates the property at issue. The transfer of property thus appears as a convergence of at least two parties in a process in which the right of the acquirer is always founded on that of the seller, who thus becomes the buyer's *auctor*. When we read in the *Digest* (50, 17, 175, 7) *non debeo melioris condicioni esse, quam auctor meus, a quo ius in me transit*, this simply means the following: "My right to property is, in a necessary and sufficient fashion, founded on that of the buyer, who 'authorizes' it." In any case, what is essential is the idea of a relationship between two subjects in which one acts as *auctor* for the other: *auctor meus* is the name given by the buyer to the current seller, who renders the property legitimate.

"The meaning of 'he who advises or persuades' also presupposes an analogous idea. It is the author who grants the uncertain or hesitant will of a subject the impulse or supplement that allows it to be actualized. When we read in Plautus's *Miles*, "*quid nunc mi auctor es, ut faciam?*," this does not simply mean, "What do you advise me to do?" It also means, "To what do you 'authorize' me, in what way do you complete my will, rendering it capable of making a decision about a certain action?"

From this perspective, the meaning of "witness" also becomes transparent, and the three terms that, in Latin, express the idea of testimony all acquire their characteristic physiognomy. If *testis* designates the witness insofar as he intervenes as a third in a suit between two subjects, and if *superstes* indicates the one who has fully lived through an experience and can therefore relate it to others, *auctor* signifies the witness insofar as his testimony always presupposes something — a fact, a thing or a word — that preexists him and whose reality and force must be validated or certified. In this sense, *auctor* is opposed to *res* (*auctor magis ... quam res ... movit*, the witness has greater authority than the witnessed thing [Liv. 2, 37, 8]) or to *vox* (*voces ... nullo auctore emissae*, words whose validity no witness guarantees [Cicero, *Coel.* 30]). Testimony is thus always an act of an "author": it always implies an essential duality in which an insufficiency or incapacity is completed or made valid.

It is thus possible to explain the sense of the term *auctor* in the poets as "founder of a race or a city," as well as the general meaning of "setting into being" identified by Benveniste as the original meaning of *augere*. As is well known, the classical world is not acquainted with creation *ex nihilo*; for the ancients every act of creation always implies something else, either unformed matter or incomplete Being, which is to be completed or "made to grow." Every creator is always a co-creator, every author a co-author. The act of the *auctor* completes the act of an incapable person, giving strength of proof to what in itself lacks it and granting life to what could not live alone. It can conversely be said that the imperfect act or incapacity precedes the *auctor*'s act and that the imperfect act completes and gives meaning to the word of the *auctor*-witness. An author's act that claims to be valid on its own is nonsense, just as the survivor's testimony has truth and a reason for being only if it is completed by the one who cannot bear witness. The survivor and the *Muselmann*, like the tutor and the incapable person and the creator and his material, are inseparable; their unity-difference alone constitutes testimony.

4.7   Let us return to Levi's paradox: "the *Muselmann* is the complete witness." It implies two contradictory propositions: 1) "the *Muselmann* is the non-human, the one who could never bear witness," and 2) "the one who cannot bear witness is the true witness, the absolute witness."

The sense and nonsense of this paradox become clear at this point. What is expressed in them is nothing other than the intimate dual structure of testimony as an act of an *auctor*, as the difference and completion of an impossibility and possibility of speaking, of the inhuman and the human, a living being and a speaking being. The subject of testimony is constitutively fractured; it has no other consistency than disjunction and dislocation—and yet it is nevertheless irreducible to them. This is what it means "to be subject to desubjectification," and this is why the witness, the ethical subject, is the subject who bears witness to desubjectification. And the unassignability of testimony is nothing other than the price of this fracture, of the inseparable intimacy of the *Muselmann* and the witness, of an impotentiality and potentiality of speaking.

Levi's second paradox, according to which "the human being is the one who can survive the human being," also finds its true sense here. *Muselmann* and witness, the inhuman and the human are coextensive and, at the same time, non-coincident; they are divided and nevertheless inseparable. And this indivisible partition, this fractured and yet indissoluble life expresses itself through a double survival: the non-human is the one who can survive the human being and the human being is the one who can survive the non-human. Only because a *Muselmann* could be isolated in a human being, only because human life is essentially destructible and divisible can the witness survive the *Muselmann*. The witness' survival of the inhuman is a function of the *Muselmann*'s survival of the human. What can be infinitely destroyed is what can infinitely survive.

4.8   Bichat's central thesis is that life can survive itself and that life is, indeed, constitutively fractured into a plurality of lives and therefore deaths. All the *Recherches physiologiques sur la vie et sur la mort* are founded on Bichat's observation of a fundamental fracture in life, which he presents as the co-presence of two "animals" in every organism. First there is the "animal existing on the inside," whose life — which he calls "organic" and compares to that of a plant — is nothing but a "habitual succession of assimilation and excretion." Then there is "the animal living on the outside," whose life — which is the only one to merit the name "animal" — is defined by its relation to the external world. The fracture between the organic and the animal traverses the entire life of the individual, leaving its mark in the opposition between the continuity of organic functions (blood circulation, respiration, assimilation, excretion, etc.) and the intermittence of animal functions (the most evident of which is that of dreaming-waking); between the asymmetry of organic life (only one stomach, one liver, one heart) and the symmetry of animal life (a symmetrical brain, two eyes, two ears, two arms, etc.); and finally in the non-coincidence of the beginning and end of organic and animal life. Just as in the fetus organic life begins before that of animal life, so in getting old and dying it survives its animal death. Foucault has noted the multiplication of death in Bichat, the emergence of a moving or detailed death, which divides death into a series of partial deaths: brain death, liver death, heart death.... But what Bichat cannot accept, what continues to present him with an irreducible enigma is not so much this multiplication of death as organic life's survival of animal life, the inconceivable subsistence of "the animal on the inside" once the "animal on the outside" has ceased to exist. If the precedence of organic life with respect to animal life can be understood as a process of development toward more and more elevated and complex forms, how is it possible to explain the animal on the inside's senseless survival?

The passage in which Bichat describes the gradual and inexorable extinction of animal life in the indifferent survival of organic functions constitutes one of the most intense moments in the *Recherches*:

> Natural death is remarkable in that it puts an almost complete end to animal life long before organic life ends. Consider man, who fades away at the end of a long period of old age. He dies in details: one after another, his external functions come to an end; all his senses cease to function; the usual causes of sensation no longer leave any impression on him. His sight grows dim, confused, and ends by not transmitting the image of objects; he suffers from geriatric blindness. Sounds strike his ear in a confused fashion, and soon his ear becomes completely insensitive to them. At this point, the cutaneous layer, hardened, covered with calluses partially deprived of blood vessels, and now inactive, allows for only an obscure and indistinct sense of touch. Habit, in any case, has blunted all sensation. All the organs that depend on the skin grow weak and die; hair and body hair grow thin. Without the fluids that nourished it, most hair falls out. Odors now leave only a light impression on his sense of smell.... Isolated in the middle of nature, partially deprived of his sensitive organs, the old man's brain is soon extinguished. He no longer perceives much of anything; his senses are almost incapable of being exercised at all. His imagination fades away and disappears. His memory of present things is destroyed; in a second, the old man forgets what was just said to him, since his external senses, which have grown weak and are, as it were, dead, cannot confirm what his spirit thinks it grasps. Ideas escape him, while the images traced by his senses no longer retain their imprint (Bichat 1986: 200–201).

An intimate estrangement from the world corresponds to this decline of external senses, an estrangement that closely recalls the descriptions of the *Muselmann* in the camps:

The old man's movements are seldom and slow; he leaves only with great cost the condition in which he finds himself. Seated beside the fire that is heating him, he spends his days concentrating on himself, alienated from what surrounds him, in the absence of desires, passions, sensations — almost without speaking, since nothing pushes him to break his silence. He is happy to feel that he still exists, for almost every other feeling has vanished.... It is easy to see, from what we have said, that in the old man external functions are extinguished one after another and organic life continues even after animal life has almost fully come to an end. From this point of view, the condition of the living being about to be annihilated by death resembles the state in which we find ourselves in the maternal womb, or in the state of vegetation, which lives only on the inside and is deaf to nature (*ibid.*: 202–203).

The description culminates in a question that is truly a bitter confession of powerlessness in the face of an enigma:

But why is it that, when we have ceased to exist on the outside, we continue to live on the inside, when senses, locomotion, and so forth are above all designed to place us in relation to bodies that nourish us? Why do these functions grow weaker than internal ones? Why is their cessation not simultaneous? I cannot succeed in fully solving this enigma (*ibid.*: 203–204).

Bichat could not have foretold that the time would come when medical resuscitation technology and, in addition, biopolitics would operate on precisely this disjunction between the organic and the animal, realizing the nightmare of a vegetative life that indefinitely survives the life of relation, a non-human life infinitely separable from human existence. But, almost as if a dark foreboding of this nightmare suddenly crossed his mind, he imagines a symmetrical possibility of a death turned upside down, in which man's animal functions survive while his organic functions perish completely:

> If it were possible to imagine a man whose death, affecting only internal functions (such as circulation, digestion, secretions, and so forth), permitted the subsistence of the set of functions of animal life, this man would view the end of his organic life with indifference. For he would feel that the worth of his existence did not depend on organic functions, and that even after their "death" he would be capable of feeling and experiencing everything that until then had made him happy (Bichat 1986: 205–206).

Whether what survives is the human or the inhuman, the animal or the organic, it seems that life bears within itself the dream — or the nightmare — of survival.

4.9   As we have seen, Foucault defines the difference between modern biopower and the sovereign power of the old territorial State through the crossing of two symmetrical formulae. *To make die and to let live* summarizes the procedure of old sovereign power, which exerts itself above all as the right to kill; *to make live and to let die* is, instead, the insignia of biopower, which has as its primary objective to transform the care of life and the biological as such into the concern of State power.

In the light of the preceding reflections, a third formula can be said to insinuate itself between the other two, a formula that defines the most specific trait of twentieth-century biopolitics: no longer either *to make die* or *to make live*, but *to make survive*. The decisive activity of biopower in our time consists in the production not of life or death, but rather of a mutable and virtually infinite survival. In every case, it is a matter of dividing animal life from organic life, the human from the inhuman, the witness from the *Muselmann*, conscious life from vegetative life maintained functional through resuscitation techniques, until a threshold is reached: an essentially mobile threshold that, like the borders of geopolitics, moves according to the progress of scientific and political technologies. Biopower's supreme ambition is to produce, in a human body, the absolute separation of the living being and the speaking being, *zoē* and *bios*, the inhuman and the human — survival.

This is why in the camp, the *Muselmann* — like the body of the overcomatose person and the neomort attached to life-support systems today — not only shows the efficacy of biopower, but also reveals its secret cipher, so to speak its *arcanum*. In his *De arcanis rerum publicarum* (1605), Clapmar distinguished in the structure of power between a visible face (*jus imperii*) and a hidden face (*arcanum*, which he claims derives from *arca*, jewel casket or coffer). In contemporary biopolitics, survival is the point in which the two faces coincide, in which the *arcanum imperii* comes to light as such. This is why it remains, as it were, invisible in its very exposure, all the more hidden for showing itself as such. In the *Muselmann*, biopower sought to produce its final secret: a survival separated from every possibility of testimony, a kind of absolute biopolitical substance that, in its isolation, allows for the attribution of demographic, ethnic, national, and political identity. If, in the jargon of Nazi bureaucracy, whoever participated in the "Final Solution" was called a *Geheimnisträger*, a keeper of secrets, the *Muselmann* is the absolutely unwitnessable, invisible ark of biopower. Invisible because empty, because the *Muselmann* is nothing other than the *volkloser Raum*, the space empty of people at the center of the camp that, in separating all life from itself, marks the point in which the citizen passes into the *Staatsangehörige* of non-Aryan descent, the non-Aryan into the Jew, the Jew into the deportee and, finally, the deported Jew beyond himself into the *Muselmann*, that is, into a bare, unassignable and unwitness-able life.

This is why those who assert the unsayability of Auschwitz today should be more cautious in their statements. If they mean to say that Auschwitz was a unique event in the face of which the witness must in some way submit his every word to the test of an impossibility of speaking, they are right. But if, joining unique-ness to unsayability, they transform Auschwitz into a reality ab-solutely separated from language, if they break the tie between an impossibility and a possibility of speaking that, in the *Muselmann*, constitutes testimony, then they unconsciously repeat the Nazis' gesture; they are in secret solidarity with the *arcanum imperii*. Their silence threatens to repeat the SS's scornful warning to the inhabitants of the camp, which Levi transcribes at the very start of *The Drowned and the Saved*:

> However the war may end, we have won the war against you; none of you will be left to bear witness, but even if someone were to sur-vive, the world will not believe him. There will perhaps be suspi-cions, discussions, research by historians, but there will be no certainties, because we will destroy the evidence together with you. And even if some proof should remain and some of you survive, people will say that the events you describe are too monstrous to be believed.... We will be the ones to dictate the history of the Lagers (Levi 1989: 11–12).

4.10   With its every word, testimony refutes precisely this isola-tion of survival from life. The witness attests to the fact that there can be testimony because there is an inseparable division and non-coincidence between the inhuman and the human, the living being and the speaking being, the *Muselmann* and the survivor. Precisely insofar as it inheres in language as such, precisely insofar as it

157

bears witness to the taking place of a potentiality of speaking through an impotentiality alone, its authority depends not on a factual truth, a conformity between something said and a fact or between memory and what happened, but rather on the immemorial relation between the unsayable and the sayable, between the outside and the inside of language. *The authority of the witness consists in his capacity to speak solely in the name of an incapacity to speak — that is, in his or her being a subject.* Testimony thus guarantees not the factual truth of the statement safeguarded in the archive, but rather its unarchivability, its exteriority with respect to the archive — that is, the necessity by which, as the existence of language, it escapes both memory and forgetting. It is because there is testimony only where there is an impossibility of speaking, because there is a witness only where there has been desubjectification, that the *Muselmann* is the complete witness and that the survivor and the *Muselmann* cannot be split apart.

It is necessary to reflect on the particular status of the subject from this perspective. The fact that the subject of testimony — indeed, that all subjectivity, if to be a subject and to bear witness are in the final analysis one and the same — is a *remnant* is not to be understood in the sense that the subject, according to one of the meanings of the Greek term *hypostasis*, is a substratum, deposit, or sediment left behind as a kind of background or foundation by historical processes of subjectification and desubjectification, humanization and inhumanization. Such a conception would once again repeat the dialectic of grounding by which one thing — in our case, bare life — must be separated and effaced for human life to be assigned to subjects as a property (in this sense, the *Muselmann* is the way in which Jewish life must be effaced for something like an Aryan life to be produced). Here the foundation is a function of a telos that is the grounding of the human being, the becoming human of the inhuman. It is this perspective that must

158

be wholly called into question. We must cease to look toward processes of subjectification and desubjectification, of the living being's becoming speaking and the speaking being's becoming living and, more generally, toward historical processes as if they had an apocalyptic or profane telos in which the living being and the speaking being, the inhuman and the human — or any terms of a historical process — are joined in an established, completed humanity and reconciled in a realized identity. This does not mean that, in lacking an end, they are condemned to meaninglessness or the vanity of an infinite, disenchanted drifting. They have not an *end*, but a *remnant*. There is no foundation in or beneath them; rather, at their center lies an irreducible disjunction in which each term, stepping forth in the place of a remnant, can bear witness. What is truly historical is not what redeems time in the direction of the future or even the past; it is, rather, what fulfills time in the excess of a medium. The messianic Kingdom is neither the future (the millennium) nor the past (the golden age): it is, instead, a *remaining time*.

4.11   In an interview in 1964 given on German television, Arendt was asked what remained, for her, of the pre-Hitlerian Europe that she had experienced. "What remains?" Arendt answered, "The mother tongue remains" (*Was bleibt? Die Muttersprache bleibt*). What is language as a remnant? How can a language survive the subjects and even the people that speak it? And what does it mean to speak in a remaining language?

The case of a dead language is exemplary here. Every language can be considered as a field traversed by two opposite tensions, one moving toward innovation and transformation and the other toward stability and preservation. In language, the first movement corresponds to a zone of *anomia*, the second to the grammatical norm. The intersection point between these two opposite currents is the speaking subject, as the *auctor* who always decides what can be said and what cannot be said, the sayable and the unsayable of a language. When the relation between norm and *anomia*, the sayable and the unsayable, is broken in the subject, language dies and a new linguistic identity emerges. A dead language is thus a language in which it is no longer possible to oppose norm and *anomia*, innovation and preservation. We thus say of a dead language that it is no longer spoken, that is, that *in it it is impossible to assign the position of a subject*. Here the already-said forms a whole that is closed and lacking all exteriority, that can only be transmitted through a *corpus* or evoked through an archive. For Latin, this happened at the time of the definitive collapse of the tension between *sermo urbanus* and *sermo rusticus*, of which speakers are already conscious in the Republican age. As long as the opposition was perceived as an internal polar tension, Latin was a living language and the subject felt that he spoke a single language. Once the opposition breaks down, the normative part becomes a dead language (or the language Dante calls *grammatica*) and the anomic part gives birth to the Romance vernaculars.

Now consider the case of Giovanni Pascoli, the Latin poet of the beginning of the twentieth century, that is, a time when Latin had already been a dead language for many centuries. In his case an individual succeeds in assuming the position of subject in a dead language, thus lending it again the possibility of opposing the sayable and the unsayable, innovation and preservation that it is by definition lacking. At first glance one could say that insofar as he establishes himself in it as a subject, such a poet genuinely resurrects a dead language. This is what happened in cases where people followed the example of an isolated *auctor*, as in the Piedmontese dialect of Forno, when, between 1910 and 1918, one last speaker passed his language on to a group of young people who began to speak it; or in the case of modern Hebrew, in which a whole community placed itself in the position of a subject with respect to a language that had become purely religious. But in this case the situation is more complex. To the degree to which a poet who writes in a dead language remains isolated and continues to speak and write in his mother tongue, it can be said that in some way he makes a language survive the subjects who spoke it, producing it as an undecidable medium — or testimony — that stands between a living language and a dead language. In a kind of philological *nekuia*, he thus offers his voice and blood to the shadow of a dead language, so that it may return — as such — to speech. Such is this curious *auctor*, who authorizes an absolute impossibility of speaking and summons it to speech.

If we now return to testimony, we may say that to bear witness is to place oneself in one's own language in the position of those who have lost it, to establish oneself in a living language as if it were dead, or in a dead language as if it were living — in any case, outside both the archive and the *corpus* of what has already been said. It is not surprising that the witness' gesture is also that of the poet, the *auctor* par excellence. Hölderlin's statement that "what remains is what the poets found" (*Was bleibt, stiften die Dichter*) is not to be understood in the trivial sense that poets' works are things that last and remain throughout time. Rather, it means that the poetic word is the one that is always situated in the position of a remnant and that can, therefore, bear witness. Poets — witnesses — found language as what remains, as what actually survives the possibility, or impossibility, of speaking.

To what does such a language bear witness? To something — a fact or an event, a memory or a hope, a delight or an agony — that could be registered in the *corpus* of what has already been said? Or to enunciation, which, in the archive, attests to the irreducibility of saying to the said? It bears witness to neither one nor the other. What cannot be stated, what cannot be archived is the language in which the author succeeds in bearing witness to his incapacity to speak. In this language, a language that survives the subjects who spoke it coincides with a speaker who remains beyond it. This is the language of the "dark shadows" that Levi heard growing in Celan's poetry, like a "background noise"; this is Hurbinek's non-language (*mass-klo, matisklo*) that has no place in the libraries of what has been said or in the archive of statements. Just as in the starry sky that we see at night, the stars shine surrounded by a total darkness that, according to cosmologists, is nothing other than the testimony of a time in which the stars did not yet shine, so the speech of the witness bears witness to a time in which human beings did not yet speak; and so the testimony of human beings attests to a time in which they were not yet human. Or, to take up an analogous hypothesis, just as in the expanding universe, the farthest galaxies move away from us at a speed greater than that of their light, which cannot reach us, such that the darkness we see in the sky is nothing but the invisibility of the light of unknown stars, so the complete witness, according to Levi's paradox, is the one we cannot see: the *Muselmann*.

4.12   The remnant is a theologico-messianic concept. In the prophetic books of the Old Testament, what is saved is not the whole people of Israel but rather only a remnant, which is indicated in Isaiah as *shear yisrael*, the remnant of Israel, or in Amos as *sherit Yosef*, the remnant of Joseph. The paradox here is that the prophets address all of Israel, so that it may turn to the good, while at the same time announcing to the whole people that only a remnant of it will be saved (thus in Amos 5:15: "Hate the evil, and love the good, and establish judgment in the gate: it may be that the Lord God of hosts will be gracious unto the remnant of Joseph;" and in Isaiah 10: 22: "For although thy people be as the sand of the sea, yet a remnant of them shall be saved").

What are we to understand here by "remnant"? What is decisive is that, as theologians have observed, "remnant" does not seem simply to refer to a numerical portion of Israel. Rather, *remnant designates the consistency assumed by Israel when placed in relation with an* eskhaton, *with election or the messianic event.* In its relation to salvation, the whole (the people) thus necessarily posits itself as remnant. This is particularly clear in Paul. In his Letter to the Romans, Paul makes use of a series of Biblical citations to conceive of the messianic event as a series of caesuras dividing the people of Israel and, at the same time, the Gentiles, constituting them each time as remnants: "Even so then at this present time also [literally 'in the time of now,' *en to nun kairo*, Paul's technical expression for messianic time] there is a remnant according to the election of grace" (Romans 11: 5). The caesuras do not, however, merely divide the part from the whole (Romans 9: 6–8: "For they are not all Israel, which are of Israel. Neither, because they are the seed of Abraham, are they all children: but, in Isaac shall thy seed be called. That is, They which are the children of the flesh, these are not the children of God: but the children of the promise are counted for the seed"). The caesuras also divide the non-people from the people, as in Romans 9: 25–6: "As he saith also in Osee, I will call them my people, which were not my people; and her beloved, which was not my beloved. And it shall come to pass, that in the place where it was said unto them, Ye are not my people; there shall they be called the children of the living God." In the end, the remnant appears as a redemptive machine allowing for the salvation of the very whole whose division and loss it had signified (Romans 11: 26: "And so all Israel shall be saved").

In the concept of remnant, the aporia of testimony coincides with the aporia of messianism. Just as the remnant of Israel signifies neither the whole people nor a part of the people but, rather, the non-coincidence of the whole and the part, and just as messianic time is neither historical time nor eternity but, rather, the disjunction that divides them, so the remnants of Auschwitz — the witnesses — are neither the dead nor the survivors, neither the drowned nor the saved. They are what remains between them.

4.13   Insofar as it defines testimony solely through the *Muselmann*, Levi's paradox contains the only possible refutation of every denial of the existence of the extermination camps.

Let us, indeed, posit Auschwitz, that to which it is not possible to bear witness; and let us also posit the *Muselmann* as the absolute impossibility of bearing witness. If the witness bears witness for the *Muselmann*, if he succeeds in bringing to speech an impossibility of speech — if the *Muselmann* is thus constituted as the whole witness — then the denial of Auschwitz is refuted in its very foundation. In the *Muselmann*, the impossibility of bearing witness is no longer a mere privation. Instead, it has become real; it exists as such. If the survivor bears witness not to the gas chambers or to Auschwitz but to the *Muselmann*, if he speaks only on the basis of an impossibility of speaking, then his testimony cannot be denied. Auschwitz — that to which it is not possible to bear witness — is absolutely and irrefutably proven.

This means that the phrases, "I bear witness for the *Muselmann*" and "the *Muselmann* is the whole witness" are not constative judgments, illocutive acts, or enunciations in Foucault's sense. Rather, they articulate a possibility of speech solely through an impossibility and, in this way, mark the taking place of a language as the event of a subjectivity.

4.14   In 1987, one year after Primo Levi's death, Zdzisław Ryn and Stanslaw Klodzinski published the first study dedicated to the *Muselmann*. The article, published in *Auschwitz-Hefte* bearing the significant title "At the Border Between Life and Death: A Study of the Phenomenon of the *Muselmann* in the Concentration Camp," contains eighty-nine testimonies, almost all of former Auschwitz prisoners. They had been asked to respond to a questionnaire on the origin of the term, the *Muselmänner*'s physical and psychological traits, the circumstances that produced "Muselmannization," the behavior of functionaries and other prisoners with respect to *Muselmänner*, and *Muselmänner*'s death and chances of survival. The testimonies collected in the article do not add anything essential to what we already knew, except for one particularly interesting point, which calls into question not simply Levi's testimony, but even one of his fundamental presuppositions. One section of the monograph (Ryn and Klodzinski 1987: 121–24) is entitled *Ich war ein Muselmann*, "I was a *Muselmann*." It contains ten testimonies of men who survived the condition of being *Muselmänner* and now seek to tell of it.

In the expression "I was a *Muselmann*," Levi's paradox reaches its most extreme formulation. Not only is the *Muselmann* the complete witness; he now speaks and bears witness in the first person. By now it should be clear that this extreme formulation — "I, who speak, was a *Muselmann*, that is, the one who cannot in any sense speak" — not only does not contradict Levi's paradox but, rather, fully verifies it. This is why we leave them — the *Muselmänner* — the last word.

I can't forget the days when I was a Muselmann. *I was weak, exhausted, dead tired. I saw something to eat wherever I looked. I dreamt of bread and soup, but as soon as I woke up I was unbearably hungry. The food I'd been given the night before (my portion of bread, fifty grams of margarine, fifty grams of jam, and four potatoes cooked with their skins on) was a thing of the past. The head of the barrack and the other inmates who had positions threw out their potato-skins, sometimes even a whole potato. I used to watch them secretly and look for the skins in the trash so that I could eat them. I would spread jam on them; they were really good. A pig wouldn't have eaten them, but I did. I'd chew on them until I felt sand on my teeth....* (Lucjan Sobieraj)

I personally was a Muselmann *for a short while. I remember that after the move to the barrack, I completely collapsed as far as my psychological life was concerned. The collapse took the following form: I was overcome by a general apathy; nothing interested me; I no longer reacted to either external or internal stimuli; I stopped washing, even when there was water; I no longer even felt hungry....* (Feliksa Piekarska)

I am a Muselmann. *Like the other inmates, I tried to protect myself from getting pneumonia by leaning forward, stretching my shoulders as much as I could and, patiently, rhythmically moving my hands over my sternum. This is how I kept myself warm when the Germans weren't watching.*

From then onward I went back to the camps on the shoulders of my colleagues. But there are always more of us Muselmänner.... (Edward Sokòl)

I too was a Muselmann, *from 1942 to the beginning of 1943. I wasn't conscious of being one. I think that many* Muselmänner *didn't realize they belonged to that category. But when the inmates were divided up, I was put in the group of* Muselmänner. *In many cases, whether or not an inmate was considered a* Muselmann *depended on his appearance.* (Jerzy Mostowsky)

Whoever has not himself been a Muselmann *for a while cannot imagine the depth of the transformations that men underwent. You became so indifferent to your fate that you no longer wanted anything from anyone. You just waited in peace for death. They no longer had either the strength or the will to fight for daily survival. Today was enough; you were content with what you could find in the trash....* (Karol Talik)

In general, one can say that among Muselmänner *there were exactly the same differences, I mean physical and psychological differences, as between men living in normal conditions. Camp conditions made these differences more pronounced, and we often witnessed reversals of the roles played by physical and psychological factors.* (Adolf Gawalewicz)

I'd already had a presentiment of this state. In the cell, I felt life leaving me. Earthly things no longer mattered; bodily functions faded away. Even hunger tormented me less. I felt a strange sweetness. I just didn't have the strength to get off my cot, and if I did, I had to lean on the walls to make it to the bucket.... (Wlodzimierz Borkowski)

In my own body, I lived through the most atrocious kind of life in the camp, the horror of being a Muselmann. *I was one of the first* Muselmänner. *I wandered through the camp like a stray dog; I was indifferent to everything. I just wanted to survive another day. I arrived in the camp on June 14, 1940, with the first transport from the Tarnow prison.... After some initial hardships, I was put in the farm-*

167

ing Kommando, where I worked at harvesting potatoes and hay and threshing until the fall of the same year. Suddenly something happened in the Kommando. They had discovered that civilians outside the camp were giving us food. I ended up among the disciplinary group, and that is where the tragedy of my life in the camp began. I lost my strength and health. After a couple of days of hard work, the Kapo of the old Kommando had me moved from the disciplinary group to the sawmill Kommando. The work wasn't as hard, but I had to stay outside all day, and that year the fall was very cold. The rain was always mixed with snow. It had already begun to freeze over and we were dressed in light fabrics — underwear and shirts, wooden clogs without socks with cloth caps on our heads. In such a situation, without sufficient nourishment, drenched and frozen every day, death left us no way out. . . . This was the beginning of the period in which Muselmannhood [das Muselmanntum] became more and more common in all the teams working outdoors. Everyone despised Muselmänner; even the Muselmann's fellow inmates. . . . His senses are dulled and he becomes completely indifferent to everything around him. He can no longer speak of anything; he can't even pray, since he no longer believes in heaven or hell. He no longer thinks about his home, his family, the other people in the camp.

Almost all Muselmänner died in the camp; only a small percentage managed to come out of that state. Thanks to good luck or providence, some were liberated. This is why I can describe how I was able to pull myself out of that condition. . . .

You could see Muselmänner everywhere: skinny, dirty figures, their skin and faces blackened, their gaze gone, their eyes hollowed out, their clothes threadbare, filthy and stinking. They moved with slow, hesitating steps poorly suited to the rhythm of the march. . . . They spoke only about their memories and food — how many pieces of potato there were in the soup yesterday, how many mouthfuls of meat, if the soup was thick or only water. . . . The letters that arrived for them from their homes didn't comfort them; they had no illusions about ever going home. Muselmänner anxiously expected packages, thinking of being full at least once. They dreamt of rummaging through the kitchen trash to find pieces of bread or coffee grinds.

Muselmänner worked out of inertia or, rather, pretended to work. For example, during my work at the sawmill, we used to look for the blunter saws that were easier to use, without worrying about whether they actually cut or not. We often pretended to work like that for a whole day, without even cutting one block of wood. If we were supposed to straighten nails, we would instead hammer away at the anvil. But we had to make sure that no one saw us, which was also tiring. Muselmänner had no goals. They did their work without thinking; they moved around without thinking, dreaming only of having a place in the line in which they'd be given more soup, more thick soup. Muselmänner paid close attention to the gestures of the food officer to see if, when he ladled out the soup, he drew it from the top or the bottom. They ate quickly and thought only about getting second helpings. But this never happened — the only ones who got second helpings were those who had worked the most and the hardest, who were favored by the food officer. . . .

The other inmates avoided Muselmänner. There could be no common subject of conversation between them, since Muselmänner only fantasized and spoke about food. Muselmänner didn't like the "better" prisoners, unless they could get something to eat from them. They preferred the company of those like themselves, since then they could easily exchange bread, cheese, and sausage for a cigarette or other kinds of food. They were afraid of going to the infirmary; they never claimed to be sick. Usually they just suddenly collapsed during work.

I can still see the teams coming back from work in lines of five. The first line of five would march according to the rhythm of the orchestra, but the next line would already be incapable of keeping up with them. The five behind them would lean against each other; and in the last

169

lines the four strongest would carry the weakest one by his arms and legs, since he was dying. . . .

As I said, in 1940 I drifted through the camp like a stray dog, dreaming of coming across at least a single potato skin. I tried to lower myself into the holes near the sawmill, where they fermented potatoes to make fodder for the pigs and other animals. The inmates would eat slices of raw potatoes smeared with saccharin, which tasted somewhat like pears. My condition grew worse everyday; I developed ulcerations on my legs and I no longer hoped to survive. I hoped only for a miracle, although I didn't have the strength to concentrate and pray faithfully. . . .

This was the state I was in when I was noticed by a commission of officers who had entered the barracks after the last roll call. I think they were SS doctors. There were three or four of them and they were particularly interested in Muselmänner. In addition to blisters on my legs, I also had a swelling the size of an egg on my ankle bone. This is why they prescribed an operation and moved me, together with some others, to Barrack 9 (which used to be Barrack 11). We were given the same food as the others, but we didn't go to work and we were allowed to rest all day long. Camp physicians visited us; I was operated on — the scars from the operation are still visible today — and I got better. We didn't have to be present at the roll call; it was warm and we were doing well. Then one day, the SS officers who were responsible for the barrack didn't come. They said that the air was suffocating and ordered all the windows to be opened. It was December, 1940. . . . After a few minutes, we were all shivering from the cold; then they made us run around in the room to heat ourselves up, until we were all covered in sweat. Then they said, "Sit down," and we did as they said. Once our bodies had cooled down, and we were once again cold, it was time for more running — and so it lasted for the whole day.

When I understood what was going on, I decided to leave. When it was time for me to be examined, I said that I was all better and that I wanted to work. And this is what happened. I was transferred to Barrack 10 (which had become number 8). They put me in a room in which there were only new arrivals. . . . Since I was an old prisoner, the head of the barrack liked me, and he spoke of me as an example for the other prisoners. . . . As a result I was transferred to the Farming Kommando, in the cowshed. There I also won the trust of the other inmates, and I had extra food, pieces of beetroot, black sugar, soup from the pig's sty, large quantities of milk and, what's more, the heat of the cowshed. This got me back on my feet again; it saved me from Muselmannhood. . . .

The period in which I was a Muselmann left a profound impression on my memory. I remember perfectly the accident in the sawmill Kommando of fall 1940; I still see the saw, the heaps of wood blocks, the barracks, Muselmänner keeping each other warm, their gestures. . . . The last moments of the Muselmänner were just as they say in this camp song:

What's worse than a Muselmann?
Does he even have the right to live?
Isn't he there to be stepped on, struck, beaten?
He wanders through the camp like a stray dog.
Everyone chases him away, but the crematorium is his deliverance.
The camp infirmary does away with him!

(Bronislaw Goscinki)

(Residua desiderantur)

Bibliography

Translator's Note: The bibliography contains only those works cited in the text. All texts have been cited from the editions listed below. In the case of foreign works that have not appeared in English, I have translated all passages from the original languages for this book.

Adorno, Theodor Wiesengrund, *Negative Dialectics*, trans. E. B. Ashton (New York: Continuum, 1973).

———, *Minima Moralia: Reflections from Damaged Life*, trans. E. F. N. Jephcott (London: Verso, 1974).

Agamben, Giorgio, *Language and Death: The Place of Negativity*, trans. Karen E. Pinkus with Michael Hardt (Minneapolis: Minnesota University Press, 1991).

Améry, Jean, *At the Mind's Limits: Contemplations by a Survivor on Auschwitz and Its Realities*, trans. Sidney Rosenfeld and Stella P. Rosenfeld (Bloomington: Indiana University Press, 1980).

Antelme, Robert, *The Human Race*, trans. Jeffrey Haight and Annie Mahler (Marlboro, VT: Marlboro Press, 1992).

Arendt, Hannah, *Eichmann in Jerusalem: A Report on the Banality of Evil* (London: Penguin, 1992).

———, *Essays in Understanding* (New York: Harcourt Brace, 1993).

Aristotle, *Metaphysics*, trans. Christopher Kirwan (Oxford, UK: Clarendon, 1993).

Bachmann, Ingeborg, *Frankfurter Vorlesungen: Probleme zeitgenössicher Dichtung* (Zurich and Munich: Piper Verlag, 1982).

Barth, Karl, *Church Dogmatics*, vol. 3: *The Doctrine of Creation*, Part 2 (Edinburgh: T. & T. Clark, 1960).

Benjamin, Walter, *One-Way Street and Other Writings*, trans. Edmund Jephcott and Kingsley Shorter (London: Verso, 1979).

Benveniste, Emile, *Problems in General Linguistics*, trans. Mary Elizabeth Meek (Coral Gables, FA: University of Miami Press, 1971).

————, *Problèmes de linguistique générale*, vol. 2 (Paris: Gallimard, 1974).

Bertelli, S., "Lex animata in terris," in *La città e il sacro*, ed. Franco Cardini (Milan: Garzanti-Scheiwiller, 1994).

Bettelheim, Bruno, *The Empty Fortress* (New York: The Free Press, 1967).

————, *The Informed Heart* (New York: The Free Press, 1960).

————, *Surviving and Other Essays* (New York: Knopf, 1979).

Bichat, Xavier, *Recherches physiologiques sur la vie et la mort* (Paris: Flammarion, 1986).

Bin, Kimura, *Ecrits de psychopathologie phénoménologique* (Paris: Presses Universitaires de France, 1992).

Binswanger, Ludwig, *Being-in-the-world: Selected Papers of Ludwig Binswanger*, trans. Jacob Needleman (New York: Basic Books, 1963).

Blanchot, Maurice, *The Infinite Conversation*, trans. Susan Hanson (Minneapolis: University of Minnesota Press, 1993).

Cardini, Franco, ed. *La città e il sacro* (Milan: Garzanti-Scheiwiller, 1994).

Carpi, A., *Diario di Gusen* (Turin: Einaudi, 1993).

Chrysostome, Jean, *Sur l'incompréhensibilité de Dieu* (Paris: Editions de Cerf, 1970).

Derrida, Jacques, *Speech and Phenomena and Other Essays on Husserl's Theory of Signs*, trans. David B. Allison (Evanston: Northwestern University Press, 1973).

Des Pres, Terence, *The Survivor: An Anatomy of Life in the Death Camps* (New York: Washington Square Press, 1976).

Felman, Shoshana and Dori Laub, *Testimony: Crises of Witnessing in Literature, Psychoanalysis, and History* (New York and London: Routledge, 1992).

Foucault, Michel, *The Archaeology of Knowledge and The Discourse on Language*, trans. A. M. Sheridan Smith (New York: Pantheon Books, 1972).

———, *Essential Works*, vol. 2: *Aesthetics, Method and Epistemology*, ed. James D. Faubion, trans. Robert Hurley and others (New York: The Free Press, 1998).

———, *Il faut défendre la société* (Paris: Gallimard-Seuil, 1997).

Frontisi-Ducroux, Françoise, *Du masque au visage* (Paris: Flammarion, 1995).

Hegel, Georg Wilhelm Friedrich, *Aesthetics: Lectures on Fine Art*, 2 vols, trans. T. M. Knox (Oxford: Clarendon Press, 1975).

Heidegger, Martin, *Bremer und Freiburger Vorträge*, in *Gesamtausgabe*, vol. 79 (Frankfurt am Main: Klostermann, 1994).

———, *Parmenides*, trans. André Schuwer and Richard Rojcewicz (Bloomington: Indiana University Press, 1992).

———, *Kant and the Problem of Metaphysics*, trans. Richard Taft (Bloomington: Indiana University Press, 1990).

Hilberg, Raul, *The Destruction of the European Jews* (New York: Harper & Row, 1979).

Kant, Immanuel, *Critique of Pure Reason*, trans. Norman Kemp Smith (London: Macmillan, 1929).

Kantorowicz, Ernst, *The King's Two Bodies: A Study in Mediaeval Political Theology* (Princeton, NJ: Princeton University Press, 1957).

Keats, John, *The Letters of John Keats*, ed. Maurice Buxton Forman (Oxford: Oxford University Press, 1935).

Kerényi, Karl, *La religione antica nelle sue linee fondamentali*, trans. Delio Cantimori (Bologna: N. Zanchelli, 1940).

Kogon, Eugen, *The Theory and Practice of Hell: The German Concentration Camps and the System Behind Them*, trans. Heinz Norden (New York: Octagon Books, 1979).

Langbein, Hermann, *Auschwitz: Zeugnisse und Berichte*, eds. H. G. Adler, Hermann Langbein, and Ella Lingens-Reiner (Frankfurt am Main: Athenäum, 1988).

———, *Menschen in Auschwitz* (Vienna: Europa Verlag, 1972).

Levi, Primo, *Ad ora incerta*, in *Opere*, vol. 2 (Turin: Einaudi, 1988).

———, "L'altrui mestiere," in *Opere*, vol. 3 (Turin: Einaudi, 1990).

———, *Conversazioni e interviste* (Turin: Einaudi, 1997).

————, *The Drowned and the Saved*, trans. Raymond Rosenthal (New York: Random House, 1989).

————, *Survival in Auschwitz and The Reawakening: Two Memoirs*, trans. Stuart Woolf (New York: Summit Books, 1986).

Lévinas, Emmanuel, *De l'évasion* (Montpellier: Fata Morgana, 1982).

Lewental, S., *Gedenkbuch, Hefte von Auschwitz* 1 (Oswiecim: Staatliches Auschwitz-Museum, 1972).

Lyotard, Jean-François, *The Differend: Phrases in Dispute*, trans. Georges Van Den Abbeele (Minneapolis: University of Minnesota Press, 1988).

Manganelli, Giorgio, *La notte* (Milan: Adelphi, 1996).

Mauss, Marcel and Henri Hubert, *Sacrifice: Its Nature and Function*, trans. W.D. Halls (Chicago, University of Chicago Press, 1964).

Pessoa, Fernando, *Always Astonished: Selected Prose*, trans. and ed. Edwin Honig (San Francisco: City Lights, 1988).

Oxford English Dictionary, 2nd ed., prepared by J.A. Simpson and E.S.C. Weiner, vol. vii (Oxford: Clarendon, 1989).

Rilke, Rainer Maria, *The Book of Hours*, trans. Stevie Krayer (Salzburg: Salzburg University, 1995).

————, *The Notebooks of Malte Laurids Brigge*, trans. Stephen Mitchell (New York: Random House, 1983).

Ryn, Zdzislaw and Stanslaw Klodzinski, *An der Grenze zwischen Leben und Tod. Eine Studie über die Erscheinung des "Muselmanns" im Konzentrazionslager*, *Auschwitz-Hefte*, vol. 1 (Weinheim and Basel: Beltz, 1987), pp. 89–154.

Satta, Sebastiano, *Il mistero del processo* (Milan: Adelphi, 1994).

Sereny, Gitta, *Into That Darkness: An Examination of Conscience* (New York: Random House, 1983).

Sofsky, Wolfgang, *The Order of Terror: The Concentration Camp*, trans. William Templer (Princeton: Princeton University Pres, 1997).

Spinoza, Baruch, *Compendium grammatices linguae hebraeae*, in *Opera*, ed. Carl Gebhardt, vol. 3 (Heidelberg: C. Winter, 1925).

Wiesel, Elie, "For Some Measure of Humanity," in *Sh'ma, A Journal of Jewish Responsibility* 5, October 31, 1975

Designed by Bruce Mau with Barr Gilmore
Typesetting by Archetype
Printed and bound by Thomson-Shore